CISSP in 21 Days

Boost your confidence and get a competitive edge
to crack the exam

M. L. Srinivasan, CISSP

BIRMINGHAM - MUMBAI

CISSP in 21 Days

First published: December 2008

Production Reference: 1121208

Published by Packt Publishing Ltd.
32 Lincoln Road
Olton
Birmingham, B27 6PA, UK.

ISBN 978-1-847194-50-3

www.packtpub.com

Cover Image by Vinayak Chittar (vinayak.chittar@gmail.com)

Credits

Author

M. L. Srinivasan

Reviewer

Jagan Rao

Acquisition Editor

Bansari Barot

Development Editor

Ved Prakash Jha

Technical Editor

Darshana D. Shinde

Copy Editor

Sneha M. Kulkarni

Editorial Team Leader

Akshara Aware

Project Manager

Abhijeet Deobhakta

Project Coordinator

Neelkanth Mehta

Indexer

Rekha Nair

Proofreader

Joel T. Johnson

Production Coordinator

Aparna Bhagat

Cover Work

Aparna Bhagat

About the Author

M.L.Srinivasan is presently the founder and CEO of ChennaiNet, an India-based technology company focused on Information Technology and Information Security related product development, services, and training. He's a Certified Information System Security Professional (CISSP) and Certified Information Security Management System Lead Auditor.

Popularly known as MLS, the author is an Information Technology and Information Security professional, with roughly 18 years of experience in various domains of IT such as Software Programming, Hardware Troubleshooting, Networking Technologies, Systems Administration, Security Administration, Information Security-related consulting, auditing, and training. MLS has been an avid trainer throughout his career and has developed many short-term and long-term training programs. One such program is "Certified Vulnerability Assessor" (cVa), which is accredited by a leading ISO certifying agency. He's a prolific speaker and has presented many papers on the Network Security domain at many international conventions and conferences.

He is a specialist IT and IS auditor with Det Norske Veritas (DNV), India region. He has performed many quality and information security audits in hundreds of medium and large organizations over the past 10 years.

He was a Technical Director with Secure Matrix, an India-based company that provides information security consulting and audits. During his tenure in the last four years, he led a team of consultants to implement many ISO 27001-certification projects across India, the Middle East, and Africa.

I would like to thank my family for all the support and, in particular, my wife who patiently proof read all the chapters.

My special thanks and gratitude goes to Mr. Jagan Rao for his critical feedback on the content.

I would like to thank the (ISC)^2 and the CISSP community for their relentless effort in spreading the information security knowledge across the world.

Last, but not the least, I would like to thank the entire team at Packt for their enthusiasm and support throughout the project.

About the Reviewer

Jagan Rao holds a Masters degree from the Indian Institute of Technology, Kharagpur.

He has a two decades of work experience in the various fields of Information Technology, particularly in the areas of Infrastructure Support, Database Management, and Information Security.

He holds the credentials of CISSP, CISM, PMP, ABCP, Oracle DBA, IBM, and HPUX System Admininstration.

He is currently working as a Manager, I.T Architecture, in an upcoming greenfield aluminium smelter (EMAL), which, on completion, is expected to become the world's largest single-site smelter.

I would like to thank my ex-colleagues, Naseeba Al Rais and Rajesh Hemrajani, for their continued support and passion that they show for infromation security related endevours.

I would also like to thank my ex-employer, Dubai Aluminium, and my current employer, Emirates Aluminium, for giving many oppurtunities and challenging assignments, particularly in the areas of Information Security.

I would like to dedicate this book to my father who is the guiding force behind everything.

Table of Contents

Preface

The Certified Information Systems Security Professional (CISSP) is an internationally recognized security qualification. Success in this esteemed exam opens the door to your dream job as an information security expert. As industry surveys show, a CISSP candidate earns a better salary than his counterparts without a security certification. In addition, the CISSP is a recognized qualification for US government jobs in the Department of Defense (DoD), and the National Security Agency (NSA). Similarly, this certification is also recognized by many governmental departments, businesses, stock exchanges, banks, and universities around the world. Therefore, obtaining this international certificate will present you with a host of opportunities, whether it is for employment, consulting, or an audit profession in the information security field.

But passing the final exam is challenging. Every year many candidates who attempt the exam do not prepare sufficiently and, unfortunately, fail at the final stage. This happens when they cover everything but do not properly review, which leads to a lack of confidence. This book will take you through the final weeks before the exam with a day-by-day plan that will cover all of the exam topics. It will help you to enter the exam room with confidence, knowing that you have done all you could to prepare for the examination day. This small, concise CISSP exam quick-revision guide provides a disciplined approach to be adopted for reviewing and revising the core concepts a month before the exam. This book provides a succinct explanation of important concepts in all 10 domains of the CISSP Common Body of Knowledge (CBK).

What this book covers

Introduction: This chapter introduces the organization of the guide, expectations, and the approach adopted.

Day 1: This chapter covers various concepts related to security management practices, control environment, and asset classification and controls.

Day 2: This chapter discusses important requirements of security awareness and training as well as risk assessment and management.

Day 3: This chapter covers the threats, vulnerabilities, and countermeasures for physical security and physical security design that includes perimeter and interior security.

Day 4: This chapter addresses the concepts in operations and facility security, along with protecting and securing equipment.

Day 5: This chapter covers concepts related to access control, methodologies and techniques, authentication, and access-related attacks and countermeasures.

Day 6: This chapter covers concepts related to vulnerability assessment and penetration testing.

Day 7: This chapter covers various concepts related to cryptography, such as methods and types of encryption, as well as the application and use of cryptography.

Day 8: This chapter covers the core concepts in Public Key Infrastructure, key management techniques, methods of cryptanalytic attacks, and various cryptographic standards.

Day 9: This chapter covers various concepts in the areas of operations procedures and responsibilities, incident management, and reporting.

Day 10: This chapter covers control environment related to operations security and also evaluation criteria, such as TCSEC.

Day 11: This chapter covers concepts in systems engineering and the Software Development Life Cycle models.

Day 12: This chapter covers IT systems, threats and vulnerabilities of application systems, and application control concepts.

Day 13: This chapter covers various concepts in network architecture, Open System Interconnect (OSI), and the TCP/IP models. It also covers various protocols in the TCP/IP models related to the application and transport layers, along with threats, vulnerabilities, attacks, and countermeasures for the TCP/IP protocols and services.

Day 14: This chapter covers different protocols that are in the network/Internet layer, data link layer, and physical layer in the TCP/IP model. In addition, it covers some of the threats and vulnerabilities that are prevalent in such protocols, common attacks, and possible countermeasures.

Day 15: This chapter covers concepts in computer architecture, the Trusted Computing Base, and protection domain and its related mechanisms.

Day 16: This chapter addresses the concepts in assurance-related standards, various certification and accreditation schemes, and various computer security models.

Day 17: This chapter covers various concepts in Business Continuity Planning, its goals and objectives as well as the concepts in the Business Impact Analysis.

Day 18: This chapter covers the Disaster Recovery Planning process, various backup concepts, and the process of resuming business from alternative sites.

Day 19: This chapter covers various computer crimes, cyber crimes, as well as different types of attacks.

Day 20: This chapter covers laws and regulations related to information systems across the world. Additionally, it covers concepts related to computer investigations and ethical usage of information systems as prescribed by international bodies including (ISC)2.

Day 21: This chapter contains a full mock test paper containing a total of 250 questions from all 10 domains.

References: This chapter provides various references and books that are relevant to the CISSP exam preparation.

Who is this book for

This book is for all the aspirants who are planning to take the CISSP examination and obtain the coveted CISSP certification, which is considered as the *gold standard* in the information security personal certification.

This book assumes that the candidate already has sufficient knowledge in all 10 domains of the CISSP CBK from work experience and knowledge gained from studying information security. This book provides a concise explanation of the core concepts that are essentially covered in the exam.

Besides being a focused guide on information security, this book is also useful as a quick reference and revision guide for System and Network Administrators, Database Administrators, System Analysts, Software Developers, Application Designers, System Architects, Legal Professionals, Security Officers, Business Continuity professionals, IT Auditors, IS Auditors, Vulnerability Assessors, Penetration Testers, and Ethical Hackers.

Conventions

In this book, you will find a number of styles of text that distinguish between different kinds of information. Here are some examples of these styles, and an explanation of their meaning.

New terms and **important words** are introduced in a bold-type font.

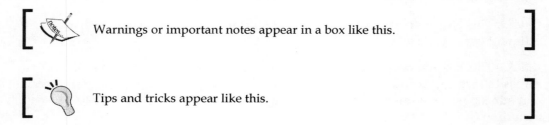

Warnings or important notes appear in a box like this.

Tips and tricks appear like this.

Reader feedback

Feedback from our readers is always welcome. Let us know what you think about this book, what you liked or may have disliked. Reader feedback is important for us to develop titles that you really get the most out of.

To send us general feedback, simply drop an email to feedback@packtpub.com, making sure to mention the book title in the subject of your message.

If there is a book that you need and would like to see us publish, please send us a note in the **SUGGEST A TITLE** form on http://www.packtpub.com or email suggest@packtpub.com.

If there is a topic that you have expertise in and you are interested in either writing or contributing to a book, see our author guide on http://www.packtpub.com/authors.

Customer support

Now that you are the proud owner of a Packt book, we have a number of things to help you to get the most from your purchase.

Errata

Although we have taken every care to ensure the accuracy of our contents, mistakes do happen. If you find a mistake in one of our books—maybe a mistake in text or code—we would be grateful if you would report this to us. By doing this you can save other readers from frustration, and help to improve subsequent versions of this book. If you find any errata, report them by visiting http://www.packtpub.com/support, selecting your book, clicking on the **let us know** link, and entering the details of your errata. Once your errata are verified, your submission will be accepted and the errata added to the list of existing errata. The existing errata can be viewed by selecting your title from http://www.packtpub.com/support.

Piracy

Piracy of copyright material on the Internet is an ongoing problem across all media. At Packt, we take the protection of our copyright and licenses very seriously. If you come across any illegal copies of our works in any form on the Internet, please provide the location address or website name immediately so we can pursue a remedy.

Please contact us at copyright@packtpub.com with a link to the suspected pirated material.

We appreciate your help in protecting our authors, and our ability to bring you valuable content.

Questions

You can contact us at questions@packtpub.com if you are having a problem with some aspect of the book, and we will do our best to address it.

1
Introduction to CISSP

Certified Information System Security Professional (CISSP) is a coveted certification for an information security professional. Certified individuals are considered experienced and knowledgeable information security professionals. This is due to the requirements for certification. To appear for the exam, a candidate should have a minimum of four to five years of relevant practical experience in two or more domains of information security.

CISSP is acclaimed as the gold standard of the security industry. The CISSP exam is conducted by the **International Information System Security Certification Consortium (ISC)²**, a non-profit consortium that is engaged in certifying information security professionals throughout their careers. The (ISC)² was founded in 1989 by industry leaders and has certified over 60,000 information security professionals in more than 120 countries.

The (ISC)² Board of Directors includes top **Information Security (IS)** professionals from a cross-section of the industry. The board members are CISSP certified and are elected, on a volunteer status, by others who have been certified.

As per (ISC)², CISSP was the first credential in the field of information security, accredited by the **ANSI (American National Standards Institute)** to **ISO (International Standards Organization)** Standard 17024:2003. CISSP certification is not only an objective measure of excellence, but a **globally recognized** standard of achievement:

- Certified Information Systems Security Professional (CISSP)
- Information Systems Security Architecture Professional (ISSAP)
- Information Systems Security Management Professional (ISSMP)
- Information Systems Security Engineering Professional (ISSEP)
- Certification and Accreditation Professional (CAPCM)
- Systems Security Certified Practitioner (SSCP)

We will be focusing on the CISSP exam in this quick revision guide.

Eligibility requirements for the CISSP exam and certification

Eligibility for obtaining this certificate is twofold:

1. **Passing the exam**:

   The exam consists of 250 multiple choice questions worth 1000 points that are to be answered in a duration of six hours. Of the 1000 points, a minimum of 700 points (70%) is required to pass this exam. The weighted value for each question varies and the distribution is not disclosed to the candidates. The exam is a written-type exam and an online test option is not offered. The (ISC)² regularly conducts the exam throughout the world. The exam schedules are available at the (ISC)² website: `http://www.isc2.org`.

2. **Professional experience**:

   Subscribing to the (ISC)² code of ethics, and showing a proof of direct professional work experience of no less than four to five years in two or more security domains, as prescribed in (ISC)² CISSP **Common Body of Knowledge (CBK)**

Those who do not have relevant experience can still appear for the CISSP exam. If they pass, (ISC)² will award them with an Associate of (ISC)² credential. Subsequently by gaining relevant years of experience, the candidate can show evidence and obtain the CISSP credential.

As per (ISC)²

The Associate of (ISC)² status is available to qualified candidates who:

- Subscribe to the (ISC)² Code of Ethics
- Pass the CISSP or SSCP certification exams based on the (ISC)² CBK, our taxonomy of information security topics.

The following information is extracted from the (ISC)² website pertaining to (ISC)² CBK .

The (ISC)² CBK is a taxonomy – a collection of topics relevant to information security professionals around the world. The (ISC)² CBK establishes a common framework of information security terms and principles, which allows information security professionals worldwide to discuss, debate, and resolve matters pertaining to the profession with a common understanding.

The (ISC)² was established in 1989, in part, to aggregate, standardize, and maintain the (ISC)² CBK for information security professionals worldwide.

Domains from the (ISC)² credentials are drawn from various topics within the (ISC)² CBK. The (ISC)² uses the CBK to assess a candidate's level of mastery of the most critical domains of information security.

The (ISC)² CBK, from which the (ISC)² credentials are drawn, is updated annually by the (ISC)² CBK Committee to reflect the most current and relevant topics required to practice the profession of information security.

The (ISC)² CBK security domains

The (ISC)² CBK for CISSP contains ten security domains. A candidate attempting the CISSP exam is tested for knowledge in these domains. The following are the ten security domains along with their key areas of knowledge:

1. **Access Control**
   - Knowledge of access control concepts, methodologies, and techniques to identify, evaluate, and respond to access control attacks such as brute force, dictionary, spoofing, denial-of-service, and so on.
   - Design, coordinate, and evaluate vulnerability and penetration tests

2. **Application Security**
   - Role of security in system life cycles
   - Application environment and security controls
   - Databases, data warehousing, threats, vulnerabilities, and protection
   - Knowledge-based systems and their security
   - Application and system related vulnerabilities and threats

3. **Business Continuity and Disaster Recovery Planning**
   - Developing and documenting project scope and plan
   - Conducting the Business Impact Analysis (BIA)
   - Developing recovery strategies
   - Training
   - Maintaining the business continuity plans

4. **Cryptography**
   - Application and the use of cryptography
   - Methods of encryption
   - Types of encryption
   - Initialization vectors
   - Cryptographic systems
   - Key management techniques
   - Message digests and hashing
   - Digital signatures
   - Non-repudiation
   - Methods of cryptanalytic attacks
   - Employing cryptographic in network security
   - Cryptography and email security
   - The Public Key Infrastructure (PKI)
   - Alternatives such as steganography, watermarking, and so on

5. **Information Security and Risk Management**
   - Understanding the organizational goals, mission, and objectives
   - Establishing governance
   - Understanding the concepts of confidentiality, integrity, and availability
   - Understanding and applying "security" concepts such as defense-in-depth, single points of failure, and so on
   - Developing and implementing security policies
   - Defining an organization's roles and responsibilities
   - Security considerations in outsourcing
   - Developing and maintaining internal service agreements
   - Integrating and supporting identity management
   - Understanding and applying risk management concepts
   - Evaluating personnel security
   - Developing and conducting security education, training, and awareness
   - Understanding data classification concepts
   - Evaluating information system security strategies

- ○ Supporting certification accreditation efforts
- ○ Designing, conducting, and evaluating security assessment
- ○ Reporting security incidents to the management
- ○ Understanding professional ethics

6. **Legal, Regulations, Compliance, and Investigations**
   - ○ Understanding common elements of international laws pertaining to information systems security
   - ○ Understanding and supporting investigations
   - ○ Understanding forensic procedures

7. **Operations Security**
   - ○ Applying security concepts such as the need-to-know/least privilege, separation of duties and responsibilities, monitoring special privileges such as operators and administrators, job rotation, marking, handling, storing and destroying of sensitive information and media, record retention, backup of critical information, anti-virus management, remote working and malware management
   - ○ Employing resource protection
   - ○ Handling violations, incidents, and breaches as well as reporting these occurrences when necessary
   - ○ Supporting high availability such as fault tolerance, denial-of-service prevention, and so on
   - ○ Implementing and supporting patch and vulnerability management
   - ○ Ensuring administrative management and control
   - ○ Understanding configuration management concepts
   - ○ Responding to attacks such as spam, virus, spyware, phishing, and so on

8. **Physical (Environmental) Security**
   - ○ Participating in site and facility design considerations
   - ○ Supporting the implementation and operation of perimeter security, interior security, operations and facility security
   - ○ Participating in the protection and security of equipments.

9. **Security Architecture and Design**
   ° Understanding theoretical concepts of security models
   ° Understanding components of information systems evaluation models
   ° Understanding security capabilities of computer systems
   ° Understanding how the security architecture is affected by covert channels, state attacks, emanations, maintenance hooks and privileged programs countermeasures, assurance, trust and confidence and the Trusted Computer Base (TCB) and its reference to monitors and kernels

10. **Telecommunications and Network Security**
    ° Establishing secure data communications
    ° Establishing secure multimedia communications
    ° Developing and maintaining secure networks
    ° Preventing attacks and controlling potential attack threats such as malicious code, flooding, spamming, and so on
    ° Remote access protocols such as CHAP, EAP, and so on

Approach

While preparing for the CISSP exam, a candidate has to read and understand many books and references. Many books cover the CISSP CBK domains in depth and provide a starting point for a thorough preparation to the exam. References to such books are covered in the references chapter at the end of this book. However, since many concepts are spread across the ten domains, it is always important to review the various concepts before the exam. This book addresses the requirements of revisiting the key concepts in these ten domains that are explained in a short, simple, and lucid form.

There are many overlapping concepts that are applicable to more than one security domain. For example, the concept of threat, vulnerability, and risk is similar and applicable to all the domains, and only the specifics will vary. Therefore, the ten security domains are aligned in a logical order so that the concepts are covered in the most appropriate sequence in this guide. A candidate can refer to this book throughout while preparing for the test or, most importantly, for a systematic review of the ten domains on a day-by-day basis, one month leading up to the exam. Therefore, the chapters are divided into 21 convenient days on the subject.

Summary

This chapter explained the eligibility requirements for the CISSP examination, the organization that is conducting the exam, the structure of the exam, information about the Common Body of Knowledge (CBK), the ten security domains prescribed in CBK, and the relevant key knowledge areas.

In the next chapter, we will explore the important concepts pertaining to information security and risk management.

2

Day1: Information Security and Risk Management

Information Security and Risk Management are analogous to each other. Information security is to preserve **Confidentiality**, **Integrity**, and **Availability (CIA)** of organizational assets. Risk management is to identify the threats and vulnerabilities that could impact the information security and devise suitable controls to mitigate these risks. We will be discussing important concepts in this domain in the next two chapters.

Knowledge requirements

A candidate appearing for the CISSP exam is expected to have broad knowledge and understanding of the following areas in the "Information Security and Risk Management" domain:

- Planning, organization, and roles of individuals in identifying and securing an organization's information assets:

  Information security is everyone's responsibility. Planning for suitable information security management practices is the first step. The planning process involves understanding the security requirements based on the business itself, and developing a suitable management framework.

  The role played by individuals in securing an organization's information assets is vital. The second step is to set up a security organization framework consisting of individuals with specific roles and responsibilities.

  Finally, the assets that need protection should be identified, and the level and type of security requirements need to be determined. Levels are based on CIA requirements and types are physical, logical, environmental, and so on. There are two important processes that help in requirement identification: asset classification and risk assessment.

Asset classification is a process that is used to group assets based on their types (for example, physical, hardware, software, paper document, and so on) and classify them based on sensitivity (for example, Confidential, Private, Public, and so on). **Risk assessment** is a process that determines the quantitative (for example, monetary value) or qualitative (for example, high, medium, low) risk value based on the type, sensitiveness, and the value of the asset.

- Development and use of policies stating management's views and positions on particular topics:

  Policies specify the management's intent on information security. For example, 'Information security policy' is a high-level document that specifies management views, intent, and support for information security throughout the organization. Other policies at department levels are developed to support high-level policies. Some such policies are **Human Resources (HR)** policy, Risk management policy, Access policy, and so on.

- Development and use of guidelines, standards, and procedures to support the policies:

  Policies only specify the management views, intent, and support. However, adherence to policy requires implementation of suitable controls. For example, access policies specify the management intent to control the access to the assets. In order to comply with the policies, suitable controls need to be implemented. Firewall or access card systems (smart card) are examples of such controls. A firewall policy or a smart card policy is a subpolicy that supports the access policy, which in turn supports the information security policy. Guidelines, standards, and procedures are developed to support the policies.

  Guidelines specify the rules or acceptable methods for implementing a policy. For example, if a firewall policy states that all incoming/outgoing traffic should be filtered to allow only authorized connections, then guidelines specify the rules and acceptable methods to be followed. For example, *Generally Accepted Principles and Practices for Securing Information Technology Systems* of NIST Special Publication 800-14 is a guideline document.

  A standard is a reference point. For example, ISO/IEC 27001:2005 is an **Information Security Management System (ISMS)** standard that can be used as a reference point for the security management program in the organization.

  Procedures support policies, guidelines, and standards. Procedures are step-by-step instructions to implement a policy, guideline, or a standard. The aim of a procedure is to achieve the desired goal through a sequence of steps.

- Security awareness training to alert employees to the importance of information security, its significance, and the specific security-related requirements relative to their position:

  Humans are the weakest link in an information security chain. Human impact on information security is vital. Security awareness training is important to mitigate risks arising out of human errors.

- Importance of confidentiality, proprietary, and private information:

  Information is a business asset and has a pivotal value in an organization. The value of information depends on various factors such as monetary value, age, useful life, and sensitiveness. Confidentiality, proprietary, and private information are classifications based on the nature of the information and its ownership. The importance of such information is based not only on the perspective of its value, but also on the perspective of legal/regulatory requirements for its protection.

- Employment agreements, employee hiring, and termination practices:

  Practices that are related to human resource management are critical for a strong information security program. Employment agreements establish the role of an individual in protecting the organization's assets and specifying the dos and don'ts. Suitable hiring and termination practices such as background checks, reference checks, segregation of duties, security clearances, access revocation, and so on are needed for ensuring information security.

- Risk management practices:

  Risk management practices include identification of risks through risk analysis and assessment, and mitigation techniques such as reduction, moving, transferring, and avoiding risks.

- Tools to identify, rate, and reduce the risk to specific resources:

  Risk is based on the probability of a threat exploiting a vulnerability and the resulting impact on the specific resource or asset. Risk analysis and assessment is a process that helps in identifying the risk, rating the risks and the controls are used for reducing the risks.

The approach

Based on the knowledge expected for the CISSP exam, this chapter is broadly grouped under four sections as shown in the following diagram:

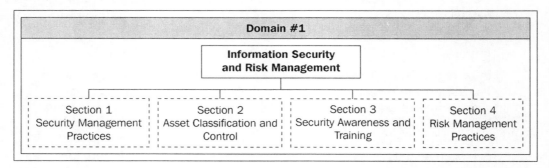

Section 1: Security Management Practices introduces various concepts, practices, and controls that are related to the day-to-day and overall management of information security in an organization.

Section 2: Asset Classification and Control covers the all-important 'asset management' practices from the information security perspective. This essentially means classifying or grouping of assets based on the criticality of the asset and devising suitable 'security controls' to maintain information security. This section also deals with classification types that are prevalent in government and private organizations.

[Unless otherwise specified, whenever the term 'Government' or 'Governmental' is used, it denotes United States Government.]

Section 3: Security Awareness and Training talks about the relevance of awareness as the most important risk mitigation strategy, as humans are considered to be the 'weakest link' in the information security chain.

Section 4: Risk Management Practices deals with the concepts in risk assessment practices such as quantitative and qualitative analyses, and risk mitigation strategies such as moving, transferring, and avoiding risks. This section also introduces the subsets of risk management practices such as Incident management, Business Continuity Planning, and Disaster Recovery Planning processes. These subsets are dealt in detail in Chapters 18 and 19.

Today we shall quickly review the concepts in the following sections:

Section 1: Security Management Practices

Section 2: Asset Classification and Control

At the end of this chapter, you should be able to explain the following topics:

- Various security management practices prevalent in the industry
- The tenets of information security
- The concept of identification, authentication, authorization, and accountability
- The control environment for information security
- Some of the Global Information Security related standards and guidelines
- Various classification types of assets and related controls used in Government and business

Security management practices

 Information security has long been considered to be purely related to **Information Technology (IT)** and its components that are technical in nature. In other words, technology-related controls are thought to be sufficient to mitigate the information security risks. However, this misconception is proved to be untrue as organizations started realizing that information security consists of management and administration related controls that may not be technical at all. For example, a firewall is a technical means of filtering traffic coming into and going out of an organization's IT network. The reason for using such a device is to allow legitimate packets of data in and out of the network and block unauthorized or malicious data from entering the internal network. Hence, it is a technical control. However, just installing a firewall may not provide a reasonable assurance in terms of security. The management based on its business objectives and information security policy determines the authorized traffic. This is a management control that specifies "what to allow". Based on the management policy, the firewall device has to be configured (fine-tuned) and needs to be monitored regularly to ensure it is working as expected (that it filters the traffic as per the policy requirement). This type of control specifies "how to allow" in the form of procedures and also monitors the implementation of the policy and its effectiveness. Hence, this type of control is called an administrative control. All three controls are required for assurance of effective information security.

Let us move on to understand the basic concepts of information security and the controls that are mentioned. In order to understand information security, we need to define the term "information". Information is a business asset that adds value to an organization. Information exists in many forms. It may be printed or written on paper, stored in electronic media, transmitted by electronic means, or passed on in conversations.

Information security management is characterized as preserving Confidentiality, Integrity and Availability (CIA) of information and related assets. These three concepts are referred to as the **tenets** of information security. The three tenets can be represented in a triangular format, and hence are called a **CIA Triad**. The following diagram illustrates the **CIA Triad**:

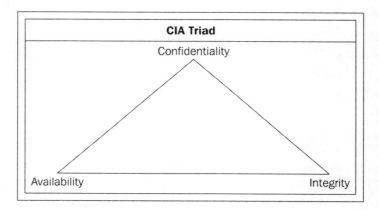

- **Confidentiality** is to ensure that the information is not disclosed to unauthorized entities.

- **Integrity** is to maintain the consistency of the information internally as well as externally. This is to prevent unauthorized modification by authorized entities.

- **Availability** is to ensure that information is available to authorized entities as and when required.

 Unless specifically defined, an entity can be personnel, a system, an application, or a process.

Every asset has a certain degree of assurance required to maintain the levels of CIA. It is not always necessary for all confidential information to be available all the time. For example, a business agreement or memorandum of understanding constitutes a legal document, and may be stored in a safe place such as a bank locker. Though the asset is highly confidential, its availability requirement is limited only to business hours. Similarly, the home page of a company web site is not confidential information, but the availability requirement is higher.

Authorized entities need to have access to the information. In order to facilitate such an access, there are two activities that come into play:

1. **Identification:** It is an entity identifying itself to the system. A common example is a username and password combination. By providing the credentials an entity is establishing its identity to the system. This concept is used in access control systems.

2. **Authentication**: When the identity information is received, the system has the ability to validate and reconcile the information provided by the entity in terms of its identity. This ability is known as authentication.

In addition to the two activities above, the system needs to ensure that the information security is assured by enforcing the following three concepts.

Once an entity is identified and authenticated, the system needs to control the access to the resources based on the entity's rights and permissions to access a particular resource. This is called **authorization** and this process determines the level of access allowed. For example a manager may have access to certain information, which a supervisor may not be allowed to access.

Once the authorization is in effect, it is important that the activities of the entity are limited to accessing the authorized resources. To ensure this, a monitoring activity is set in place. The activity of monitoring an entity's behavior in the system is known as **accountability**. Access logs and audit trails are some of the examples of this activity.

Most importantly, even when an authorized entity accesses the information, the level of confidentiality requirement of that information determines the actions that can be performed on the information. Whether the information can be copied, printed, or forwarded to third parties, and so on is determined by the confidentiality requirements. This requirement is known as **privacy**.

All the above concepts and activities form the basis of information security management. In order to ensure that these activities perform as expected, various checks and balances are introduced. These checks and balances are termed as **control environment**. We now move on to understand the control environment pertaining to security.

Control environment

The basis of a control environment is risk management. Based on the security risks that an organization faces, suitable controls are devised and deployed to mitigate such risks. A risk is a function of **probability** of a security event happening and the **consequence** of such an event, and risk is characterized by threats and vulnerabilities.

Human loss would have been a disastrous consequence to the hurricane event "Gustav". One of the controls here is evacuation. However, long term controls could be predictability, containing global warming, and so on.

- **Threat** is an event that could compromise the information security by causing loss or damage to the assets. For example, a hurricane is a threat.
- **Vulnerability** is a hole or weakness in the system. For example, not having hurricane-proof infrastructure is vulnerability.
- Threat can exploit vulnerabilities through its agents called as **threat agents**.
- A **security control** is a defined activity or a mechanism that is designed to ensure information security all times. Ensuring information security means preserving CIA of information assets.

The primary objective of a control is to mitigate risks arising out of threats and vulnerabilities. At the macro level, there are three types of controls that are prevalent in organizations.

Management controls

Management controls are characterized to state the views of the management and its position on particular topics.

Information security policy is a management control policy wherein the management provides its views as well as support and direction for security.

Administrative controls

While a policy is a high-level document that shows the intent of the management, administrative controls are used to implement such policies.

Procedures, guidelines, and standards are administrative controls that support the policies.

Technical controls

Since information is stored and processed predominantly in IT systems, technical controls are used to support the management and administrative controls by technical means.

Firewall, Intrusion Detection Systems, Intrusion Prevention Systems, anti-spam, anti phishing, antivirus, and so on are examples of technical controls.

Besides these three broad levels of controls to ensure that information is secure, the following four types of controls are used as countermeasures to mitigate the risk arising out of the vulnerability exploitations in a system:

1. **Preventative controls** are to prevent security violations. Examples include vulnerability assessment and patch management.

2. **Corrective controls** are to ensure that a successful attack may not have an adverse impact on the systems. For example, isolating affected systems, switching over to alternative network, and so on.

3. **Detective controls** are to detect a security violation, such as intrusion in time, so as to apply a countermeasure. Intrusion detection systems work as detective controls.

4. **Deterrent controls** are to deter an attack. These controls are devised to increase the work factor required for an unauthorized access or attack. High rise walls, cameras, barbed fences, entry point with two-point checks and dogs are some of the deterrent controls from the physical security perspective.

 Work factor is the amount of time or effort required to accomplish an attack. The greater the factor, the greater the difficulty.

Standards and guidelines

There are many standards and guideline documents published by standards agencies such as the **National Institute of Standards** and **Technology (NIST)**, **International Organization** for **Standardization (ISO)** and so on, which provide guidance for information security management. Some standards and guidelines, along with their core intent are listed here.

NIST special publication 800-14

Generally Accepted Principles and Practices for Securing Information Technology Systems is NIST's special publication which elaborates the concept of **System Security Life Cycle**. There are five phases in this life cycle, which are as follows:

- Initiation phase: To express the need and document the same
- Development/acquisition phase: Design and development, purchasing as well as programming are accomplished here

- Implementation phase: Testing and installation of the systems
- Operation/maintenance phase: As the name implies, the systems are operated and modified as per the requirements
- Disposal phase: Retiring obsolete systems along with secure disposal are accomplished here

ISO/IEC 27000

The **International Organization** for **Standardization (ISO)** along with the **International Electrotechnical Commission (IEC)** has published two important standards for **Information Security Management Systems (ISMS)**. They are:

- ISO/IEC 27002 (Code of practice for information security): This standard provides a list of best practices an organization can adopt for security management. These best practices are grouped under 11 security domains. This standard was earlier known as ISO/IEC 17799.
- **ISO/IEC 27001:** This standard specifies the management framework required for information security, and is a certifiable standard in the sense that an organization can seek certification against this standard for the information security management systems. This standard was earlier known as BS7799.

Security posture

Security management includes three components. First is policies, procedures, and guidelines. Second is security awareness and training. The third is risk management. These three define an organization's security initiatives and program, which in turn defines the **security posture** of the organization.

Asset classification and control

Information security is the preservation of CIA of an organization's assets. The level of security assurance required is determined by the type of asset and its value.

Information is a business asset that adds value to an organization. Asset classification identifies the type of information asset based on the value, sensitivity, and degree of assurance required. This enables us to devise suitable controls.

The following concepts are applicable to information assets:

- **Classification criteria**—Information assets are generally classified based on their value, age, useful life, and personnel association based on privacy requirements.

- **Owner**—The owner of the information is responsible for its protection. The owner plays the role of determining the classification level, periodical review, and delegation.

- **Custodian**—A custodian is the one delegated by the owner to maintain the information. A custodian's role includes backup and restoration of the information and maintaining the records.

- **User**—A user is the person who uses the information. A user may be an employee, an operator, or any third party. The role of a user is to exercise due care while handling the information by following the operating procedures. The user is responsible for using the information only for authorized purposes.

Classification types in government

Governmental agencies classify information based on the confidentiality requirements. It is also based on the damage that might be incurred if the information is disclosed or compromised. The classification schema also enforces the "need to know" principle for access. A Need-to-know restriction denotes that certain information is restricted for access even when the entity has access approvals. The entity has to establish a specific need to know that access to such restricted information is necessary for conducting official duties. The following is a list of potential classifications:

- **Top Secret** information is that which will cause exceptional damage to national security if disclosed to unauthorized entities. This is a Level 5 or highest-level classification.

- **Secret** information which is disclosed without authorization has the potential to cause serious damage to national security. This is one level down from top secret.

- **Confidential** information could cause certain damage to national security when disclosed to unauthorized entities. This is Level 3 classification.

- **Sensitive but unclassified** is a type of information that may not cause damage to national security.

- **Unclassified** information does not compromise confidentiality and its disclosure will not have adverse impacts. This information is neither confidential nor classified.

Classification types in private sector

Private and public sector entities classify information under four categories which are as follows:

- **Confidential** is the classification used to denote that the information is to be used strictly within the organization. Its unauthorized disclosure will be a liability. This is the highest level of classification in the private sector.

- **Private** is an information classification that is applicable to personnel information and should be used strictly within the organization. The compromise or unauthorized disclosure will adversely affect the organization. This is Level 3 classification.

- **Sensitive** is a classification used to ensure higher confidentiality and integrity requirements of the information asset.

- **Public** is an information classification applicable to all the information that can be disclosed to everyone. However, unauthorized modifications are not allowed. This is the lowest level of classification.

Summary

Today we've revised some of the main concepts in the domain "Information Security and Risk Management".

In a nutshell, preserving CIA of information assets is the core focus of information security, while risk management focuses on the ways to maintain this core focus. Security management is based on robust and established practices. Controls are necessary to establish and maintain security, and international standards and guidelines are available to be used as a best practice specification for a suitable control environment. Finally, we've observed that asset classification and the related controls are important to establish suitable confidentiality, integrity, and availability levels for the assets and to establish necessary controls.

Tomorrow we'll focus on the importance of training and awareness and its role in information security management. We'll also focus our attention on some of the important concepts in risk management practices that are prevalent in the industry.

Practice questions

1. Which of the following is a correct description of Information Security?

   a) Information security is protection of confidentiality, integrity and availability

   b) Information security is disclosure of confidentiality, integrity and availability

   c) Information security is preservation of confidentiality, integrity and availability

   d) Information security is prevention of confidentiality, integrity and availability

2. The system's ability to validate and reconcile the information provided by the entity in terms of its identity is known as _____.

   a) authorization

   b) authentication

   c) identification

   d) privacy

3. Which one of the following is used to show the management's intent to provide direction and support for information security?

   a) Security policy

   b) Security procedure

   c) Security awareness

   d) Security guideline

4. Which one of the following phase comes as the fourth phase in the logical order pertaining to the system security life cycle?

   a) Implementation phase

   b) Disposal phase

   c) Operation/maintenance phase

   d) Development/acquisition phase

5. Which one of the following is a common type of classification in Government as well as private/public sector organizations?

   a) Top Secret

   b) Confidential

   c) Unclassified

   d) Public

3

Day 2: Information Security and Risk Management

Yesterday we focused on the important concepts in information security areas such as Security Management Practices, Control Environment, and Asset Classification and Control.

Today we'll move on and discuss the importance of security awareness and training in information security. We'll look at recommendations from various standards including NIST's recommendations for establishing, administering, and maintaining a suitable security awareness and training program; training-related best practices as prescribed in ISO/IEC 27002. We'll also discuss various important concepts in risk assessment and management practice that can be considered as the backbone of information security.

Security awareness and training

The information security domain consists of many concepts and definitions. Also, information security initiatives in an organization will have many policies, procedures, and technology components. In order to have an effective security within the organization, it is important for the people, or personnel, to be aware of the security requirements, the organization-specific security policies and procedures, and most importantly, the specific roles and responsibilities of the personnel pertaining to security.

Security awareness and training is one of the core components of the risk management program in any organization. The objective is to ensure that the personnel are aware of the security requirements and are trained to handle day-to-day security events.

Security awareness requirements in national and international standards

Security awareness is an important aspect for an effective security program in an organization. The National and International standards emphasize this as well with clearly defined methodologies. Let us briefly look at couple of them.

NIST publication 800-14

NIST's special publication *Generally accepted principles and practices for securing information technology systems*, an American national standard recommends seven steps for a security awareness and training program. These seven steps can be divided into three broad areas of the program such as identification, management, and evaluation.

- In the **identification** phase, an organization would establish scope, goals and objectives, training staff identification, and the audience

- In **managing** the program, an organization would motivate the management and employees; administering as well as maintaining the program

- Periodically, an organization will **evaluate** the program for its effectiveness

ISO/IEC 27002:2005 information technology— security techniques—code of practice for information security management

This is an acknowledged international standard that provides some of the best practices in various domains of information security. The following are some of the good practices a security professional should be aware of, which are related to security awareness and training:

- Based on their job function, the standard emphasizes that all employees, and where relevant, the contractors and the third-party users, should be provided with appropriate awareness training as well as regular updates in organizational policies and procedures.

- The employee induction program should consist of awareness training that covers the organization's security policies and security expectations. The personnel should undergo such training before any access to information or services is granted to them.

- The training program should contain the security requirements of the organization, legal responsibilities and business controls, and most importantly, correct usage instructions that relate to information-processing facilities.

- Procedures related to log-on, appropriate usage of systems, networks, software packages, and also an explanation of disciplinary processes in case of policy or procedure violations should be part of the training.

- The training should also focus on known threats in order to enhance awareness on security incidents and problems and provides ways to respond to them based on the personnel's role.

Identifying security awareness needs

As evident from the standards above, it is imperative that security awareness needs must be established for a proper training program. The following pointers should be considered while establishing security awareness needs are based on the following:

- **Business Requirements** such as the necessity to protect information. For example, non-disclosure agreements with the customers, criticality of the information assets, and so on.

- **Legal/Regulatory/Statutory Requirements**. For example, privacy laws, data protection acts, cyber laws, and so on.

- **Security policies** of the organization. For example, information security policy, access control policy, acceptable use of assets, and so on.

- **Incident classification** and **management**.

Coverage of security awareness training

Based on the security awareness needs, an organization should, at the minimum level, consider the following topics for the awareness training programs:

- Security roles and responsibilities
- Compliance with security policies, standards, and procedures
- Commitment of senior management
- Acceptable-use policies
- Desktop security
- Log-on requirements
- Password administration guidelines

- Social engineering
- Policies and procedures to prevent social engineering attacks
- Incident-handling procedures
- Understanding interdependency of controls such as managerial, operational or administrative, and technical controls
- User and administrator training in methods, procedures, and security
- Use of software packages
- Mobile computing and tele-working related policies and procedures
- Legal responsibilities and business controls
- Information on the disciplinary process
- Business continuity processes relevant to the personnel
- Post-incident/crisis management processes

Awareness training on incidents

An information security incident is an event that breaches a safeguard or a control. For example, a computer virus that goes undetected by an anti-virus software is an incident. If an incident is not responded to within a reasonable time frame, it may manifest to a larger extent and cause severe damage to the IT environment. Awareness about incidents, and the way to respond to them, is an important part of a training program.

The following information security events or incidents are worth considering for the awareness training program:

- Loss of service, equipments, or facilities
- System malfunction or overload
- Human errors
- Non-compliance with policies or guidelines
- Breaches of physical security arrangements
- Uncontrolled system changes
- Malfunction of software or hardware
- Access violations

Measuring security awareness maturity in terms of benefit/value

Measurements helps in reducing the frequency and severity of security-related issues. Measurements that could help in such a process are as follows:

- Expectations from the data privacy requirements or confidentiality requirements is a good starting point. Measuring the level of awareness and knowledge about privacy requirements and confidentiality requirements of data is a key to this.

- Reduction in number of incidents.

- Increased reporting of security incidents and security weaknesses from the users.

- Lesser non-conformities during internal and external audits.

- Consistent and expected behavior during emergencies.

- Broader understanding of security issues.

- Awareness of the surroundings particularly when out of the office.

- Non-susceptible to social engineering attacks.

Risk assessment and management

Risk, as defined by a dictionary, is to "Expose to a chance of loss or damage". There are many types of risks an organization faces in its day-to-day business functions.

In order to understand the risk, one needs to properly understand assets, threats, and vulnerabilities.

Risk has to be understood from the following perspectives

- **Risk to What?** Risks are generally to the assets. (See the next paragraph on assets which gives categorization and examples of such assets).

- **Risk from What?** A risk can be from many threat sources such as earthquakes, floods, hackers, fires, viruses, disgruntled employees, and so on.

- **Risk of What?** There is damage when an asset is compromised by a threat. The damage can be monetary loss, image loss, customer loss, or legal issues. Due to this, the organization may be at risk of loosing money, loosing a customer, or of facing legal/regulatory consequences.

Assets

An **asset** can be a hardware, software, process, product, or infrastructure that has a value to an organization and needs protection.

Assets can be grouped as follows:

- **Physical assets** are tangible in nature and their examples include buildings, furniture, **Heating**, **Ventilating** and **Air Conditioning (HVAC)** equipments, and so on.

- **Hardware assets** are also tangible in nature, but are related to computer and network systems. Examples include servers, desktop computers, laptops, routers, network cables, and so on.

- **Software assets** are intangible (though they may be stored in a hard disk or CD) assets for which an organization owns a license to use. This effectively means the organization does not have **Intellectual Property Rights (IPR)** over such assets. Examples include **Operating Systems (OS)**, **Data Base Management Systems (DBMS)**, Office Applications, Web Server Software, and so on.

- **Information assets** are intangible in nature (though the storage medium may be physical such as note books, ledgers, CDs, hard drives, tapes, and so on). They are owned by the organization. Examples include business processes, policies and procedures, customer information, personnel information, agreements, formulas developed in-house or outright purchased, and so on.

- **Personnel assets** are people associated with the organization such as employees, contractors, third-party consultants, and so on.

All these types of assets in the organization are used for business purposes and have certain value attached to them. The value can be monetary or of great organizational importance. A compromise to such assets will have an impact in terms of monetary loss or customer loss, or legal/regulatory non-compliance.

From the information security perspective, all these assets have a requirement of assuring a certain level of CIA.

Threat

A **threat** is an event that could compromise the information security by causing loss or damage to assets. A threat is predominantly external to an organization. Examples of a threat include fire, flood, hacking, etc.

Vulnerability

A **vulnerability** is a hole, or weakness, in the system. A threat can exploit vulnerabilities through its agents known as **threat agents**. For example, having no anti-virus software is a vulnerability, which a threat, such as a virus, could exploit. Similarly, hacking is a threat that could exploit a weakness in the system through its agent, a cracker (hacker with a malicious intent).

Risk

When a threat exploits a vulnerability, it results in a **security violation**. A security violation may be defined as a threat event that exploits a vulnerability, which in turn compromises a security control. This compromise may affect the CIA requirement of an asset. The damage caused due to a security violation is known as the **impact**. In other words, the magnitude of such an impact is known as **risk**. If the magnitude of an impact can be calculated in monetary terms (say, a dollar value), then the risk is defined in quantitative terms. If the magnitude cannot be determined in terms of monetary value and can be measured in relative terms (such as high, low, medium), then the risk is defined in qualitative terms.

Risk definitions

International standard ISO/IEC 27001 defines the following risk-related terminologies that are provided from the ISO/IEC Guide 73:

Risk — A combination of the probability of an event and its consequence

Risk analysis — The systematic use of information to identify sources and to estimate the risk

Risk evaluation — The process of comparing the estimated risk against a given risk criteria to determine the significance of the risk

Risk assessment — The overall process of risk analysis and risk evaluation

Risk treatment — The process of selection and implementation of measures to modify the risk

Risk management — The coordinated activities to direct and control an organization with regard to risk. This typically includes risk assessment, risk treatment, risk acceptance, and risk communication.

Risk acceptance — The decision to accept the risk

Risk appetite — The amount and type of risk an organization is prepared to pursue or take

Risk scenarios

Risk, in terms of information security, is defined as the **probability** of a threat exploiting a vulnerability in the system, and the **consequence** of loss or damage to an asset due to that event.

There are four scenarios of the probability x consequence analysis:

- Probability is low and the consequence is low
- Probability is low and consequence is high
- Probability is high and consequence is low
- Probability is high and consequence is high

Risk assessment

By systematically analyzing the probability of a threat exploiting a vulnerability and the related consequences, one can deduce the risk. This process is known as **risk analysis**. The process of determining the risk level in terms of threats and vulnerabilities, and the probability versus consequence analysis is known as **risk assessment**. An assessment is a process in which many related parameters are taken into consideration to derive a value which could be a number (quantitative) or an expression (qualitative). For example, an insurance agent may consider different parameters such as age, health conditions, hereditary diseases, habits, and so on before determining a premium for life insurance. Similarly, risk assessment is a systematic exercise that considers various parameters (threat, vulnerabilities, impacts, and so on) pertaining to the asset to derive a risk value.

Once the risks are identified, it is important to devise strategies to mitigate them. These strategies are known as **controls** or **countermeasures** and termed as **safeguards** against the risk. There are four types of risk mitigation strategies followed in the information security domain:

- Risk acceptance
- Risk reduction
- Risk transfer
- Risk avoidance

Suitable controls are devised to mitigate the risks. The overall process of risk identification, analysis, assessment, and mitigation is known as **risk management**.

The following figure illustrates the risk assessment and risk management principles:

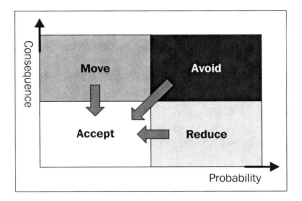

The risk analysis process involves two distinctive activities. One is to identify the probability of occurrence and the other is to measure the impact of risk. In other words, the analysis process tries to estimate the loss in terms of monetary value if a risk materializes. However, assets can be both tangible and intangible in nature. It is not possible to always determine the value of assets in monetary terms. Therefore, two types of analyses are used for loss expectancy. One is called quantitative risk analysis and the other is called qualitative risk analysis.

In **quantitative risk analysis**, an assessment is done to identify the risk in terms of numeric values such as monetary loss.

In **qualitative risk analysis**, the risk assessment uses certain predefined ratings to arrive at risk levels.

Both quantitative and qualitative risk analysis processes require that the value of the asset be determined.

Quantitative risk assessment

When a threat event happens, the percentage of loss of an asset is based on its exposure level to that particular threat. This percentage is called the **Exposure Factor (EF)** of that asset.

When a monetary value, or a dollar value, is assigned in terms of the expected loss due to a single threat event, then it is called **Single Loss Expectancy (SLE)**.

Single Loss Expectancy is the **Asset Value (AV)** multiplied by the **Exposure Factor (EF)**. In other words, **SLE = AV x EF**.

The estimated frequency, or probability, of a threat event occurring is known as the **Annualized Rate of Occurrence (ARO)**.

When SLE is multiplied by ARO, the resulting value is called **Annualized Loss Expectancy (ALE)**.

ALE is a dollar figure that may be treated as a financial loss.

 Even after applying the controls, it may not be possible to assure either 100% security or 0% risk to the assets. There is an amount of risk that remains after implementing the safeguards. This risk is called as **residual risk**.

Qualitative risk assessment

A qualitative risk assessment tries to provide an estimated potential loss or risk in qualitative terms such as high, medium, low, or any other suitable terms.

The following table illustrates the results of a qualitative risk assessment:

Probability	Consequence	Risk
High	High	High
High	Low	Medium
Low	High	Medium
Low	Low	Low

Summary

In this chapter we looked at various requirements pertaining to Security Awareness and Training. This included concepts related to risk and assessment techniques such as risk determination from threats and vulnerability, the impact of security violation, and the concepts of quantitative and qualitative risk analysis methods. We've also focused on risk management techniques from the perspective of probability and consequence analysis.

Tomorrow we move on to an important security domain that deals with the physical security aspects that a professional needs to be aware of.

Practice questions

1. In order to have an effective security within the organization, it is important that the people or personnel are aware of _____.

    a) Security requirements

    b) Security policies and procedures

    c) Roles and responsibilities

    d) All of the above

2. The probability of a threat exploiting the vulnerability in the system, and the consequence of loss or damage to an asset due to that event is termed as _____.

    a) Threat

    b) Vulnerability

    c) Risk

    d) Safeguard

3. Which of the following is correct?

    a) Qualitative risk analysis is to qualify the risk and quantitative risk analysis is to measure the same.

    b) Qualitative risk analysis is to qualify the risk and quantitative risk analysis is to monitor the same.

    c) Qualitative risk analysis provides intangible values while quantitative risk analysis provides tangible values.

    d) Qualitative risk analysis is to quantify the risk and quantitative risk analysis is to measure the same.

4. Single Loss Expectancy multiplied by Annualized Rate of Occurrence is the _____.

    a) Exposure Factor

    b) Annualized Loss Expectancy

    c) Asset Value

    d) Risk level

5. The risk that remains after implementing a safeguard is the _____.

    a) Relative risk

    b) Quantitative risk

    c) Residual risk

    d) Qualitative risk

4

Day 3: Physical (Environmental) Security

In the last two chapters we have looked at general security management practices as well as fundamental concepts associated with risk assessment and management. Today and tomorrow, we'll look at "Physical Security" domain, which is easier to perceive than other domains.

The physical security domain consists of risks to physical assets that are specific to infrastructure as well as to components that are tangible in nature. This domain addresses threats and vulnerabilities that are prevalent and could affect the security in terms of CIA. A security professional needs to be aware of the threats, vulnerabilities that pose risks, as well as countermeasures that are available to mitigate them.

The physical security domain consists of two distinctive areas pertaining to the protection requirements. The first distinctive area is related to the security along the boundaries of the physical infrastructure. This is termed as **perimeter** security. The term perimeter is also used in computer networking. In that context it means the logical boundaries of a network. In physical security domain, perimeter depicts the physical boundary.

The second distinctive area is related to the physical protection of assets within the boundaries, which is known as **interior** security. While designing controls for physical security, professionals need to consider the security requirements as well as the best options available to them to meet such requirements.

Knowledge requirements

A candidate appearing for the CISSP exam is expected to have a broad knowledge and understanding of the following areas in the physical security domain:

- Participate in the site and facility design considerations
- Support the implementation and operation of perimeter security
- Support the implementation and operation of interior security
- Support the implementation and operation of operations/facility security
- Participate in the protection and securing of equipment

The approach

Based on the knowledge you are expected to have for a CISSP exam, this chapter is broadly grouped under four sections as shown in the following diagram:

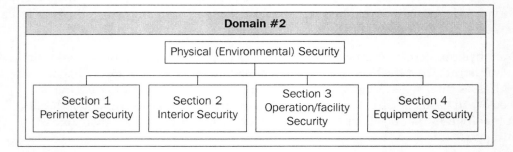

Section 1: **Perimeter Security** deals with the security considerations for preventing and controlling access to the physical premises. This essentially is concerned with the security at the physical boundary level.

Section 2: **Interior Security**, as the name implies, is about security requirements within the premises. This section is concerned with detecting unauthorized intrusions, security issues due to fire, electrical power, and other environmental factors such as humidity, temperature, and so on.

Section 3: **Operations/facility Security** pertains to administrative and auditing controls that are necessary to ensure secure operations.

Section 4: **Equipment Security** addresses the requirements of security controls pertaining to computing equipments from the physical security perspective. One of the primary considerations is equipment theft protection.

Today we will review some of the common threats, vulnerabilities to physical security, and the types of physical security controls. So let's quickly review the concepts related to the following:

Section 1: Perimeter Security

Section 2: Interior Security

Threats, vulnerabilities, and countermeasures for physical security

We have seen the concept of threats and vulnerabilities in the previous chapter. Though threats are predominantly common across most of the security domains, the vulnerabilities they could exploit will vary along with the countermeasures which are specific to them. The following are some of the threats that could exploit the vulnerabilities in the infrastructure (note that infrastructure includes IT infrastructure as well) and its associated components.

Common threats

Some of the common threats to physical environment are as follows:

- Theft
- Heat and temperature
- Humidity
- Organic materials and chemicals that are in gaseous or liquid form
- Organisms such as microbes
- Missiles or bombs that are used as projectiles
- Natural calamities such as earthquakes, floods, and so on
- Electrical power disruptions that includes electro-magnetic interference

Common vulnerabilities

The vulnerabilities that could be exploited, from the threats just mentioned, include, but are not limited to, the following:

- Lack of physical entry controls and lack of accountability
- Lack of fire extinguishers or improper maintenance
- Improper or poor cabling

- Inappropriate chemicals used in the fire extinguishers for the protection of a particular type of asset
- Inappropriate storage of magnetic media
- Weak access controls and intrusion detection systems
- No backup or business continuity plans
- Lack of power control systems
- Lack of awareness

While a deeper understanding of these threats and vulnerabilities is essential to do a proper risk assessment, it is important to understand some of the specifications that pertain to to the equipments and physical security standards while designing the appropriate countermeasures.

Physical security design

While designing a robust physical security environment, a security professional needs to take into account the following three important parameters:

1. Physical facility
2. Geographic operating location
3. Supporting facilities

The National Institute of Standards and Technology (NIST) Special Publication 800-12: *An Introduction to Computer Security – The NIST Handbook* explains the three parameters as follows.

Physical facility

The **physical facility** is usually the building, other structure, or vehicle housing the system and network components.

Systems can be characterized based on their operating location as static, mobile, or portable.

Static systems are installed in structures at fixed locations.

Mobile systems are installed in vehicles that perform the function of a structure, but not at a fixed location.

Portable systems are not installed in fixed operating locations.

Geographic operating location

The facility's general **geographic operating location** determines the characteristics of natural threats, which include earthquakes and flooding; man-made threats such as burglary, civil disorders, or interception of transmissions and emanations; and damaging nearby activities including toxic chemical spills, explosions, fires, and electromagnetic interference from emitters such as radars.

Supporting facilities

Supporting facilities are those services (both technical and human) that underpin the operation of the system. The system's operation usually depends on supporting facilities such as electric power, heating and air conditioning, and telecommunications. The failure, or substandard performance, of these facilities may interrupt operation of the system and may cause physical damage to system hardware or loss of stored data.

The design should consider the following three primary requirements in terms of security:

- **Unauthorized disclosure** leading to confidentiality breach
- **Loss of control** over the integrity of the information
- **Interruptions** as well as physical damage that could affect availability

Also, one of the most important threats that needs to be considered for physical security is **theft** as this could affect all the three.

Physical security controls

The following types of controls need to be considered for the design:

Preventative controls: They are designed to prevent a **security event**. For example, having a high-rise wall will be a control to prevent intrusion.

[**Security event**: It is an undesirable activity that could affect confidentiality, integrity, or availability of the information asset.]

The following examples are preventive-physical controls:

- High-rise wall
- Fences
- Locks

Detective controls: These controls are designed to detect an event before it could damage the facility.

The following examples are detective-physical controls:

- Fire alarm
- Intrusion detection systems such as a motion or heat sensor
- Surveillance monitors such as CCTV

Reactive controls: These controls are designed to react in a timely manner to a security event. For example, an armed response to an intrusion.

The following examples are reactive-physical controls:

- Armed response
- Mantrap systems

Deterrent controls: These controls are designed to act as deterrents against an attempt to breach the security. For example, guards and dogs will deter unauthorized entry.

The following examples that are deterrent-physical controls:

- Guards
- Dogs
- Lighting

Perimeter security

Perimeter security relates to the security considerations pertaining to boundaries. Securing, the entry and exit points of the facility, networks, and so on will fall under perimeter security.

In the physical security domain, the following controls are applicable to perimeter security:

Guards are a form of security control to prevent, detect, deter, and react to an intrusion event. They also act as a physical access control to the facility. The ability to adapt to situations is a major plus to this type of security. The disadvantages are related to their availability in hostile environments that do not support human intervention, reliability, as well as cost.

Dogs are a type of security control to prevent, detect, deter, and react to an intrusion event. But where a judgment is necessary, their ability is limited.

Fencing is an access control for perimeter security. High-rise walls, gates, mantraps, and turnstiles are some examples. The following are some of the height requirements pertaining to fencing:

- A 3' to 4' high fence deters casual trespassers
- A 6' to 7' high fence is too hard to climb easily
- A 8' high fence with 3 strands of barbed wire deters most intruders

Turnstile is a type of fencing that will allow only one person to pass through it at a time, and is also known as a **baffle gate**.

Perimeter Intrusion Detection and Assessment System (PIDAS) uses a fencing system to detect intrusion and raise an alarm as well.

Locks are preventative access control to perimeter security. **Preset locks** have preset internal mechanisms, while **programmable locks** have dials that can be programmed to contain digits or letters, or combination of both.

Lighting is a deterrent control. The purpose of lighting is to discourage intruders as well as to detect suspicious movements. NIST standards specify an illumination of two-feet wide and eight-feet high for critical areas.

Closed Circuit Televisions (CCTV), as well as **heat sensors,** are some of the devices that are used to monitor the facilities.

Access control devices such as **access cards** control physical access to the facility.

Access cards can be categorized as photo cards, digitally encoded cards, and also wireless cards. When an access card combines the physical and logical access control, as well as contains embedded integrated circuits that can process information, then it is known as a **smart card**.

Biometric devices use the physical characteristics of the person to identify and provide access to the facility. Some examples are finger print scanners, retina scanning, and so on.

Interior security

Interior security refers to the security considerations pertaining to the facilities that are inside the perimeter. These will include equipments inside the data center and personnel working in such facilities.

One of the most important aspects of interior security is the threat posed by unauthorized intrusions, fire, electrical power, and **Heating, Ventilation** and **Air Conditioning (HVAC)**.

Unauthorized intrusions

Unauthorized intrusions to the interior of a facility is controlled by motion detectors, man-trap, and so on.

Motion detectors are used in interior security to detect suspicious movements. They raise an alarm based on the type of motion detection technique used.

Man-trap systems are designed to stop and trap an intruder between two entrances. Based on physical access control mechanisms, a man-trap becomes activated upon detection of suspicious movement either automatically or manually.

Motion detectors

Wave pattern is a type of motion detector that would generate an alarm when the wave pattern is disturbed. There are three types of sensors used in wave-pattern motion detectors. They are passive infrared, ultrasonic, and microwave.

When an electric field is used around an object being monitored and the field gets charged, so as to raise an alarm, it is known as **capacitance** based motion detectors.

Audio detectors are a type of motion detector that passively listen to abnormal sounds to detect motion.

Fire

Fire is a threat that could damage the physical assets such as computers, networks, and the data center.

Fire spreads through **combustible materials**. While fire extinguishers or suppression agents are used to contain the rapid spread of fire, a professional has to be cautious about the type of extinguishing material used.

Fire classes

For the fire to catch and spread, a combustible material is required. A fire is classified into four classes based on the type of combustible material involved.

The **National Fire Protection Association** (**NFPA**) provides the following specifications regarding fire classes based on the type of combustible material and the suppression mediums.

- **Class A** combustible materials are wood, paper, cloth, and rubber. Most of the plastics also fall into this class
- **Class B** combustible materials are oils, greases, oil-based paints, lacquers, flammable liquids, and gases
- **Class C** is predominantly electrical equipments that are energized
- **Class D** refers to flammable chemicals such as magnesium and sodium

Fire detectors

Fire detectors are controls for detecting and responding to heat, flame, or smoke. Depending upon the type of detection, they can be classified as heat sensors, flame sensors, or smoke sensors.

Fire suppression mediums

Water, Soda acid, Carbon dioxide (CO_2), and **Halon** are examples of the fire suppression mediums.

Portable fire extinguishers predominantly use CO_2 or Soda acid.

Halon is a suppressing medium that is no longer allowed to be used as it has been designated as an ozone-depleting substance.

Water sprinklers

Fire extinguishers use either a water sprinkler or a gas discharger to suppress the fire.

There are four types of water sprinklers. They are as follows:

- **Wet pipe** sprinkling systems always contain water and the valve opens when the heat rises above 165° F
- **Dry pipe** sprinkling systems work in such a way that water flows from the outer valve when the heat rises above the threshold level
- **Deluge** sprinkler systems are used to discharge large volumes of water
- **Preaction** combines wet as well as dry pipe systems such that the water flow is controlled

Gas dischargers

Gas discharge systems use CO_2 or halon instead of water, and are usually used under the raised floor of the data centers.

Electrical power

Clean **electrical power** is a requirement for equipment to function properly. If the power is not clean, it will result in spoiling or damaging the equipment. This may result in the malfunctioning of devices leading to unavailability and corruption of data.

The following are the most important terms that are related to electrical power that could affect equipment:

- When the power fluctuates due to interference, the effect is called **noise**.
- When there is a charge difference between neutral, hot, and ground electrical wires, it results in **Electromagnetic Interference (EMI)**. This interference is caused by electromagnetic waves.

Radio Frequency Interference (RFI) is caused by radio waves generated by the electrical system components such as cables, florescent lights, and so on.

The following are definitions related to electrical power that a candidate should be thoroughly acquainted with:

- **Fault** — A momentary power loss
- **Blackout** — A complete power loss
- **Sag** — A momentary low voltage
- **Brownout** — A low voltage for a prolonged period of time
- **Spike** — A temporary high voltage
- **Surge** — A high voltage for a prolonged period of time
- **Inrush** — An initial high amount of incoming power
- **Noise** — A steady interference
- **Transient** — An interference of short duration
- **Clean** — Non-fluctuating power

Humidity is the percentage of water vapor present in the air. For computer systems to function properly, the humidity levels should be between 40 and 60 percent.

If humidity is more, water condensation will spoil the computer parts, and if the humidity is less than static electricity will affect the computer parts.

Summary

In this chapter we've reviewed some of the common threats, vulnerabilities, and related countermeasures pertaining to the physical security domain. More importantly, our focus was to understand different controls such as preventive, detective, reactive, and deterrent that are applicable to the physical security domain and few examples associated with each of them.

We've dealt with the concept of perimeter security as well as interior security while focusing on some of the standard specifications. These standards include the height of walls, recommended illumination levels, types of fire extinguishers, the types of materials used, and concepts related to electrical and magnetic disturbances.

We'll move ahead and look into the concepts that are related to operations/facility security, and physical and environmental security considerations for protecting and securing equipments tomorrow.

Practice questions

1. Which of the following needs to be considered while designing controls for physical security?

    a) Physical facility
    b) Geographic operating location
    c) Supporting facilities
    d) All of the above

2. An undesirable activity that could affect Confidentiality, Integrity, or Availability of information asset a(n) _____.

    a) Threat
    b) Vulnerability
    c) Risk
    d) Security Event

3. Which one of the following is called as a "baffle gate"?

    a) High-rise walls
    b) Gates
    c) Turnstiles
    d) Electric fence

4. According to the National Fire Protection Association, which of the following is a Class D fire class?

    a) Wood, paper and cloth
    b) Greases and flammable liquids
    c) Flammable chemicals such as sodium
    d) Water

5. When the voltage is low for a prolonged period of time, it is known as a _____.

    a) Noise
    b) Blackout
    c) Brownout
    d) Sag

5

Day 4: Physical (Environmental) Security

In the last chapter we covered some of the concepts pertaining to the physical security domain focusing on threats, vulnerabilities, and countermeasures, including a brief overview of different controls.

Today we'll focus on operations/facility security that is relevant to the management of facilities and related controls. We'll also focus on the importance of equipment protection and some of the best practices in the physical protection of data storage mediums.

Operations/Facility security

Facility security is concerned with the management of facility controls. The important controls that need attention have to do with auditing and procedures that need to be followed during an emergency.

Auditing

Auditing is a process to check and validate the effectiveness of controls. The primary tool that assists the audit is an audit trial. In the physical security domain, auditing is done primarily from the scope of physical access controls. The focus of the audit is to ascertain that the threats and vulnerabilities to physical access have been identified; and that suitable mitigation to the risks is being implemented and the effectiveness of physical access controls is ascertained.

While doing audits within the scope of physical security of information systems, the following points need to be considered:

- The physical location of the information systems needs to be examined. Environmental factors such as proximity to toxic chemical installations, locations that are in the seismic zone (regions where earthquakes are known to occur) and close to the seashore at best can be avoided.

- Heat, Ventilation, and Air Conditioning (HVAC) specifications for server and network equipments should be adhered to along with their proper functioning and maintenance. It is better not to have windows in the data center, and the doors are designed to maintain positive air pressure (implies that the air flows out of the room when the door is opened).

- The usage of raised floors in the data centers under which all the cables and ducts are run.

 Based on various specifications, a data center's raised floor can be anywhere between 300 mm to 800 mm depending on the floor area.

- Access control mechanisms are important to check the adequacy of such controls. The usage of smart cards, proximity cards, biometric sensors, and mantrap systems for data center access control should be encouraged.

- Periodic vetting of personnel working in critical installations such as data centers.

- Access controls to support infrastructure such as telecommunication rooms, power control rooms housing UPS and batteries, and so on.

- Fire detection and suppression controls based on the recommended specifications.

- Adequacy of lighting and emergency lighting.

- Adequacy of water, temperature, humidity sensors, and their alarm functions.

- Avoiding obvious sign boards and directions to critical installations.

- Insurance coverage.

An **audit trail** contains all the recorded events. The events may be security related or general activities. One of the most important audit trails in physical security is the access details to the data center and other control rooms. The access details should contain access attempts, the result such as success or failure, and also the location accessed.

The record of access events are stored in a file known as a **Log**. **Access logs** contain the events that are related to access attempts and **error logs** contain the exceptions.

Generally, access logs contain event-related details such as the date and time of access attempt, the result of the access attempt in terms of success or failure, the location where the access was granted, the person who was authorized, and the modifications to the access privileges.

Emergency procedures

Physical security also deals with procedures that need to be followed during emergencies. An emergency is an undesired event that may disturb the operations for a prolonged period of time. The impact of an emergency event could be devastating in terms of human loss, facility, connectivity, equipment, and data loss. Proper procedures need to be developed, personnel should be trained on such procedures, and they should be periodically tested for effectiveness and continued usability.

The following sections deal with emergency procedures that an information security professional should be aware of.

Startup and shutdown procedures

During an emergency the IT systems may be shut down intentionally, may need to be relocated to a different site, or the data may be moved to a different system at a remote site. System **startup** and **shutdown procedures** contain guidelines and activities that need to be performed in such a way that security could not be compromised during system or data migration or relocation. These procedures should include emergency procedures to address the requirements when a disaster strikes. Some of the startup and shutdown procedures include the following:

- Checking all the cables before the startup to ensure that they are not loose
- Checking that the power strip is turned on and the power plug is tightly placed
- Checking that peripheral devices are properly connected and powered on as per the procedures
- Booting the systems to a single-user or multi-user mode as per the security requirements
- Activating network connections in a manual or an automatic mode based on the security requirements
- Ensuring that the system shuts down completely during a system halt

- Avoiding physical reset of the operating system

- Ensuring that all the programs are closed before the shutdown

- In the case of an unplanned or unexpected shutdown, ensuring that the system is restarted in a diagnostic mode such that any data corruption is checked before loading the operating system

Evacuation procedures

Evacuation procedures address priorities in terms of evacuating assets from the disaster-struck site and the proper handling of such assets. Personnel are the first to be secured during an emergency or a disaster. It is important that evacuation procedures first address the secure evacuation of personnel.

The following points should be considered while developing and testing the evacuation procedures:

- Emergency exits should be clearly marked and should lead to an open space

- A floor plan with clear marking of emergency locations and indicating the current location should be available in all strategic locations

- Emergency lights should be installed at strategic locations throughout the facility

- A clearly marked assembly area needs to be identified or created, and personnel should be advised to assemble and remain in the assembly area during the evacuation

- Automatic shutdown of equipments such as air conditioners during a fire alarm should be considered

- Equipments such as fire extinguishers should be available at strategic locations

- The maintenance of fire extinguishers must be up-to-date

- Trained personnel designated as wardens or supervisors, who should direct and control emergency procedures, should be available

- Roles and responsibilities of building wardens or supervisors, along with other subwardens should be clearly defined, and their action plans, including coordination, should be documented clearly

- Identification mechanisms such as different-colored helmets or coats should be used in order to identify relevant support personnel

Training and awareness

Training and awareness play important roles during emergencies. Most importantly, the personnel need to be aware of the emergency procedures. To achieve this, organizations should conduct periodic **mock tests** to ensure the activities that need to be performed during an emergency or disaster are rehearsed and any deviances are documented. These mock tests allow the security planners to fine-tune the emergency procedures, and that percolates into the training activities. The periodical mock tests are also known as **evacuation drills**.

The following points should be covered in training and awareness programs, as well as evacuation drills:

- The evacuation drills should be periodically conducted
- The success and failures during such drills should be properly documented and the lessons learned from such exercises should be updated in the emergency procedures and training manuals
- An explanation of different alarm types should be given
- An explanation of different identification mechanisms for support personnel should be given
- Actions to be taken by personnel when the alarm signals should be mentioned
- The location of assembly points should be mentioned
- Security procedures should be followed if computer equipments are moved

Protecting and securing equipments

Physical security is also concerned with the physical protection of equipments and in addressing various security requirements pertaining to the media where data is stored.

Theft is one of the most important threats that needs to be addressed for personal computers, laptops, or media protection.

Equipment security

Cable locks are used to physically secure PCs and laptop computers. These locks prevent the computer or laptops to be detached and taken away.

Encryption is used to make the folders and files secure such that unauthorized disclosure and modification is prevented.

Full disk encryption is used to encrypt the data in laptops. This is to ensure that even if the laptop is lost, the contents are not disclosed. This method is also used to ensure that the system is not compromised using a technique known as **cold boot attack**.

 A cold boot attack is used to retrieve information such as password or encryption keys from the DRAM memories even after the power is removed. This is due to the data remanence property of DRAM memories.

Modern technologies include a security token to control access to the laptop as well as remote laptop security mechanisms which enable the owner to disable the laptop access remotely, such as through the Internet.

Port protection is used to ensure that the media devices such as CD-ROM, floppy drive, and **Universal Serial Bus (USB)** devices such as memory stick, **Wireless-Fidelity (WI-FI)** ports, printers, and scanners are not accessible to the unauthorized personnel. The purpose of port protection is to prevent the downloading or transferring of confidential information or intellectual property by unauthorized users to a portable medium.

Switches are used to prevent a malicious user from powering the systems on and off.

BIOS checks use password protection during the boot up process to control access to the operating system. These checks are called **pre-boot authentication**.

Secondary storage devices such as **Hard Disk Drives (HDD)** and display devices such as computer monitors, as well as other hardware equipments, are prone to failure due to various factors such as vibration, electrical fluctuation, electro-magnetic interference, etc. For critical systems such as servers, high availability is a primary requirement. There are two important parameters that are used in the IT industry to qualify server grade equipments.

One parameter is **Mean Time Between Failure (MTBF)**. An MTBF is a time measurement that specifies an average time between failures. This time is known as the useful life of the device.

The other parameter is **Mean Time To Repair (MTTR)**, which indicates the downtime or the average time required to repair the device.

Media security

Storage media such as hard disks, backup taps, CDs, and diskettes need additional security measures to ensure security of the data they contain. The controls should prevent data disclosure and modification by unauthorized entities.

The following controls need to be considered for media security:

Storage controls are the primary means to protect the data in storage media such as hard disk, magnetic tapes, CDs, etc. The primary consideration should be controlling access to the data, which is usually achieved by encrypted keys. Additional security considerations are required when the backup media is stored off-site.

Maintenance is a regular process to ensure that the data in the storage media is not corrupted or damaged. Media handling procedures are used to ensure this.

Proper **usage instructions** for handling the media should be provided to the users and operators.

Media usage should be in accordance with the established policies and procedures.

Data destruction is done by way of formatting the media. One-time formatting may not completely delete all data. Formatting the media seven times for complete data destruction is recommended by some of the standards. **Degaussing** is another effective method of destroying the data in magnetic media.

Data remanence is the residual data that remains when the data is not completely erased or destroyed. When the media is reused, this may result in an unauthorized disclosure of sensitive information. It is a good practice to prevent **media reuse** by physically destroying the media completely. In case of reuse, there should be policies and procedures to ensure that the data is destroyed completely.

Summary

In this chapter, we covered some of the considerations from the information security perspective in terms of operations and the facilities. In addition, we also covered the requirements pertaining to the protection of equipments and the security considerations for equipments.

In the next chapter we'll focus on the important security domain of "Access Control" that deals with controlling access to information and facilities.

Practice questions

1. Which of the following is not an audit control?
   a) Audit trial
   b) Access log
   c) Cable lock
   d) Error log

2. Evacuation procedures should primarily address _____.
   a) Network
   b) Furniture
   c) People
   d) Computers

3. Which of the following is a port protection control?
   a) Physically securing the laptops by cable
   b) Degaussing the hard disk drive
   c) Securing the media devices by controlling the access
   d) Destroying the media

4. Data remanence is _____.
   a) Data that is in the media before erasure
   b) Data that remains after data erasure
   c) Data that is reused
   d) Data that is newly created

5. Degaussing is not a method to _____.
   a) Completely erase the contents in the media
   b) Destroy the media
   c) Ensure that no residual data remain after erasure
   d) Prevent data remanence

6

Day 5: Access Control

Access control, as the name implies, is the domain that deals with controlling access to information and the associated information system assets such as computers, networks, data center, etc. As with the overall objective of information security, access control is to preserve the CIA of information assets by way of administrative, technical (logical), and physical controls.

There are many threats and vulnerabilities pertaining to information system access that pose a risk to information security. Lack of access control mechanisms would allow an unauthorized entity to have access to information processing facilities and to the information that needs protection.

Knowledge requirements

A candidate appearing for the CISSP exam should have knowledge in the following areas that relate to access control:

- Control access by applying concepts, methodologies, and techniques
- Identify, evaluate, and respond to access control attacks such as Brute force attack, dictionary, spoofing, denial of service, etc.
- Design, coordinate, and evaluate penetration test(s)
- Design, coordinate, and evaluate vulnerability test(s)

The approach

In accordance with the knowledge expected in the CISSP exam, this domain is broadly grouped under five sections as shown in the following diagram:

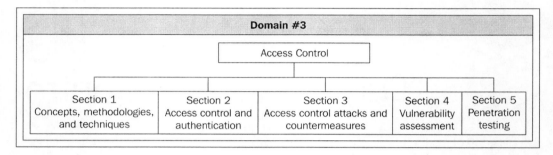

Section 1: The **Access Control** domain consists of many concepts, methodologies, and some specific techniques that are used as best practices. This section covers some of the basic concepts, access control models, and a few examples of access control techniques.

Section 2: Authentication processes are critical for controlling access to facilities and systems. This section looks into important concepts that establish the relationship between access control mechanisms and authentication processes.

Section 3: A system or facility becomes compromised primarily through unauthorized access either through the front door or the back door. We'll see some of the common and popular attacks on access control mechanisms, and also learn about the prevalent countermeasures to such attacks.

Section 4: An IT system consists of an operating system software, applications, and embedded software in the devices to name a few. Vulnerabilities in such software are nothing but holes or errors. In this section we see some of the common vulnerabilities in IT systems, vulnerability assessment techniques, and vulnerability management principles.

Section 5: Vulnerabilities are exploitable, in the sense that the IT systems can be compromised and unauthorized access can be gained by exploiting the vulnerabilities. Penetration testing or ethical hacking is an activity that tests the exploitability of vulnerabilities for gaining unauthorized access to an IT system.

Today, we'll quickly review some of the important concepts in the Sections 1, 2, and 3.

Access control concepts, methodologies, and techniques

Controlling access to the information systems and the information processing facilities by means of administrative, physical, and technical safeguards is the primary goal of access control domain. Following topics provide insight into some of the important access control related concepts, methodologies, and techniques.

Basic concepts

One of the primary concepts in access control is to understand the **subject** and the **object**.

A **subject** may be a person, a process, or a technology component that either seeks access or controls the access. For example, an employee trying to access his business email account is a subject. Similarly, the system that verifies the credentials such as username and password is also termed as a subject.

An **object** can be a file, data, physical equipment, or premises which need controlled access. For example, the email stored in the mailbox is an object that a subject is trying to access.

Controlling access to an object by a subject is the core requirement of an access control process and its associated mechanisms. In a nutshell, a subject either seeks or controls access to an object.

An access control mechanism can be classified broadly into the following two types:

1. If access to an object is controlled based on certain contextual parameters, such as location, time, sequence of responses, access history, and so on, then it is known as a **context-dependent** access control. In this type of control, the value of the asset being accessed is not a primary consideration. Providing the username and password combination followed by a challenge and response mechanism such as **CAPTCHA**, filtering the access based on MAC adresses in wireless connections, or a firewall filtering the data based on packet analysis are all examples of context-dependent access control mechanisms.

    Completely Automated Public Turing test to tell Computers and Humans Apart (CAPTCHA) is a challenge-response test to ensure that the input to an access control system is supplied by humans and not by machines. This mechanism is predominantly used by web sites to prevent Web Robots (WebBots) to access the controlled section of the web site by brute force methods.

The following is an example of CAPTCHA:

2. If the access is provided based on the attributes or content of an object, then it is known as a **content-dependent** access control. In this type of control, the value and attributes of the content that is being accessed determines the control requirements. For example, hiding or showing menus in an application, views in databases, and access to confidential information are all content-dependent.

Access control models

Access control models define methods by which a system controls the access to an object by a subject. The following are some of the models that are predominantly used in the access control domain.

Discretionary access control

Discretionary access control is a control in which the subject has some authority to specify the objects that are accessible to it. In simpler terms, access to an asset is based on the discretion of the owner of the asset.

Access Control List (ACL) is an example of discretionary access control, wherein users and privileges are mapped. The following is a simple example of an ACL that allows or denies a connection from a specific IP addresses by a router:

> 10 permit 10.1.1.1
>
> 20 permit 10.1.1.2
>
> 30 permit 10.1.3.0, wildcard bits 0.0.0.255

In this example, the router allows connections from 10.1.1.1, 10.1.1.2, and all IP addresses in the 10.1.3.0 to 10.1.3.255 range, and denies any other connections.

Identity based access control is a form of discretionary access control in which the control is based on an individual's identity. For example, biometrics based access control systems are based on this type.

Non-discretionary access control

When the access to an object is based on certain rules, it is known as a **Rule Based Access Control (RBAC)**. For example, the clearance level of the subject and the classification level of the object determine the access levels. A practical examples includes your college providing Internet access during specific hours of the day. The rule here is based on time.

When the access is controlled based on mandatory rules, it is known as a **Mandatory Access Control (MAC)**. This type of access control is based on security labels. The security label is applicable to a subject as well as an object. A subject should have an equal or a higher level of security label than the object to access it. For example, most of the modern day operating systems such as Vista or certain Linux variants, restrict permissions of applications to access certain process based on integrity or sensitiveness labels.

The acronym **MAC** is also used in computer networking and it denotes **Media Access Control**. This is an addressing scheme that provides a unique hardware number to the communication cards.

Trusted Computer System Evaluation Criteria (TCSEC) defines mandatory access control as "a means of restricting access to objects based on the sensitivity (as represented by a label) of the information contained in the objects and the formal authorization (for example, clearance) of subjects to access information of such sensitivity". TCSEC is explained in detail in the *Operations Security* Chapter on Day 10.

If a centralized authority controls the access based on a specific policy, then the same is known as a **non-discretionary access control.**

Centralized access control is a facility in which all the core functions for access such as **Authentication, Authorization,** and **Accountability (AAA)** are performed from a centralized location.

A **Role Based Access Control (RBAC)** is a non-discretionary access control based on the subject's role or position in the organization. A majority of applications such as **Enterprise Resource Management (ERP),** and **Manufacturing Execution Systems (MES)** use this control as a default or preferred access control.

Rule Based Access Control (RBAC) and Role based Access Control (RBAC) share the same acronym, RBAC.

A **task based access control** is based on a subject's responsibilities in the organization.

A **lattice-based access control** is one where there are a pair of values that determine the access rights. The pair values are related to the least upper bound and the greatest lower bound in the lattice model. This is another type of non-discretionary access control. This model is usually represented in a grid-like setup where a subject and object are mapped.

In the following example, **User Levels** and **File levels** are mapped in a lattice model to represent access levels:

	File1	File2	File3	
User3	RW	RW	RW	Sensitivity
User2	RW	RW	No Access	
User1	RW	No Access	No Access	

User Levels

De-centralized access control, or **distributed access control**, are the examples where the core functions of access are distributed over a network. A distributed database is an example of such system.

Access control and authentication

As we saw in *Chapter 2 Information Security And Risk Management*, the access control process consists of two distinctive activities. One is related to the "identification" of the subject by the system and the other is "authentication", which is the system's ability to validate the credential supplied by the subject.

The authentication process may require more than one type of credential to validate the identity. This is known as **factoring**. Access control security is greater when more than one factor of authentication is used.

When an entity, or subject, is validated against a single credential, it is known as **single-factor authentication**. For example, providing a username and password to the system is a single-factor authentication. Generally, the username and password combination authenticates the credentials from "**what you know**" (the username and password).

When an entity, or subject, is validated against two different credentials, then it is known as **two-factor authentication**. For example, providing a PIN along with the ATM or smart card to the system is a two-factor authentication. In this scenario, the system authenticates the credentials from "**what you have**" (a smart card) and "what you know" (a PIN number).

When an entity, or subject, is validated against three different credentials, then it is known as **three-factor authentication**. For example, providing a PIN along with the ATM or smart card and also a swiping you finger to the finger print reader (biometric), the reader is a three-factor authentication. In this case, the system authenticates the credentials from "**what you are**" (finger print), "what you have" (a smart card), and "what you know" (a PIN number).

 Biometric authentication validates biological characteristics to authenticate the entity or user. This follows the principle "what you are". Examples of biometric authentication methods include fingerprint scanning, retina scanning, hand geometry, and face geometry.

Access control attacks and countermeasures

There are many types of attacks that can be attributed to compromising access control systems and processes to gain unauthorized access. The following are some of the prominent ones.

Port scanning and compromise

Backdoors are the open ports created by malicious programs that allow an unauthorized entity to gain access into the system. An important countermeasure is to periodically check the open ports in the system and close any ports that are not in use by authorized programs. Port scanning tools will help in this process.

Denial-of-Service (DoS) is a type of attack wherein the legitimate users of the system are prevented from access by the reduction of availability. A **Distributed Denial of Service (DDoS)** is a type of attack where multiple systems attack a single resource from distributed locations. SYN attacks, Teardrop attack, Smurf are some of the examples of a DOS attack. A countermeasure for DoS attacks is through the regular monitoring of network activities.

Hijacking

Hijacking is an attack in which the session established by the client to the server is taken over by a malicious person or process. Strong session management and encryption is the countermeasure for such attacks.

The **Man-in-the-Middle-attack** is a type of attack where an attacker hijacks the established session by the client to the server by substituting his public key for the client's.

TCP hijacking is a type of attack in which the TCP session of the trusted client to the server is hijacked by an attacker.

Malicious code

There are many **malicious codes**. The basic functionality of malicious code is to execute itself in the client machine and compromise the security. An important countermeasure is to use and update the anti-virus systems, the firewall, and intrusion detection systems.

A **Trojan horse** is a type of malicious code that comes disguised inside a trusted program. Once installed, this malicious code can open ports, create backdoors to the system, and do innumerable security breaches. When the Trojan horse is activated on a particular event (such as a particular date), it is known as a **logic bomb**.

Malicious mobile codes are executed in the client system through the network from a remote server.

Password attacks

Password guessing is one of the attacks that use various methods to obtain the users' passwords. Use of a strong password with a combination of alphanumeric and special characters is a helpful countermeasure. Also, adhering to strict password policies such as frequent password changes, length of passwords, history of passwords are effective against such attacks.

Dictionary attacks are a type of password-guessing attack that check the encrypted password database with words found in a dictionary.

Brute force attacks are the means by which the password database is attacked with all types of letters and combinations.

Hybrid attacks combine the dictionary as well as brute force attacks.

Replay attacks are the ones in which the session (like authentication) is captured and replayed against the system.

Vulnerability compromises

Scanning is an attack that probes the network and system to identify vulnerabilities for planning a possible attack to compromise.

Vulnerability exploitation is a way of attacking systems by compromising the holes, or errors in the operating system or application software, to gain access or bypass the security controls.

Spoofing is a type of attack to imitate a trusted entity, thereby making the system trust this imitated entity. IP spoofing is an example of such an attack.

Social engineering is a type of attack to obtain credential information such as passwords, PIN numbers, and so on. by using social skills such as impersonation, fake emails, and so on.

An important countermeasure to vulnerability compromises in systems is to periodically scan and fix the vulnerabilities in the IT systems using vendor-supplied patches as well as other means of filtering and protection by using suitable vulnerability management tools.

Summary

In this chapter we first looked at some of the fundamental access control related concepts, methodologies, and techniques such as RBAC, MAC, as well as centralized and de-centralized access controls.

We've also reviewed some of the authentication concepts in terms of factored authentication.

There are quite a number of attacks such as brute force, spoofing, denial-of-service, etc., which may compromise the access control systems. We've reviewed some of these attacks and their corresponding countermeasures.

Tomorrow we'll focus on vulnerability and penetration test(s) that gives us a way to identify weaknesses in the systems and to protect the system against these weaknesses.

Practice questions

1. Which one of the following is not a Mandatory Access Control?

   a) Rule based access control

   b) Role based access control

   c) Lattice based access control

   d) Discretionary access control

2. If access to an object is controlled based on parameters such as location, time, etc., then this type of access control is known as _____.

   a) Content-dependent access control

   b) Context-dependent access control

   c) Character-dependent access control

   d) Class-dependent access control

3. Which one of the following is called as a logic bomb?

   a) Spoofing

   b) Trojan horse getting activated on an event

   c) Vulnerability exploitation by an attacker

   d) Virus

4. Dictionary attack is a type of?

   a) Denial of Service attack

   b) Spoofing

   c) Password guessing attack

   d) Social engineering

5. The basic functionality of a malicious code is to _____.

   a) Upgrade the operating system

   b) Execute itself in the client system

   c) Spoof

   d) Denial of Service

7
Day 6: Access Control

IT components such as operating systems, application software, and even networks, have many vulnerabilities. These vulnerabilities are open to compromise or exploitation. This creates the possibility for penetration into the systems that may result in unauthorized access and a compromise of confidentiality, integrity, and availability of information assets.

Vulnerability tests are performed to identify vulnerabilities while penetration tests are conducted to check the following:

- The possibility of compromising the systems such that the established access control mechanisms may be defeated and unauthorized access is gained
- The systems can be shut down or overloaded with malicious data using techniques such as DoS attacks, to the point where access by legitimate users or processes may be denied

Vulnerability assessment and penetration testing processes are like IT audits. Therefore, it is preferred that they are performed by third parties.

The primary purpose of vulnerability and penetration tests is to identify, evaluate, and mitigate the risks due to vulnerability exploitation.

Today we'll focus on IT vulnerabilities, the impact due to compromise, and the overall cycle of vulnerability and penetration tests. We'll also discuss some of the emerging standards in terms of vulnerability naming systems such as **Common Vulnerabilities and Exposures (CVE)**, which is a dictionary for vulnerability names; and **Common Vulnerability Scoring System (CVSS)**, as defined by the National Institute of Standards and Technology (NIST).

Vulnerability assessment

Vulnerability assessment is a process in which the IT systems such as computers and networks, and software such as operating systems and application software are scanned in order to indentify the presence of known and unknown vulnerabilities.

Vulnerabilities in IT systems such as software and networks can be considered **holes** or **errors**.

These vulnerabilities are due to **improper software design, insecure coding**, or both. For example, **buffer overflow** is a vulnerability where the boundary limits for an entity such as variables and constants are not properly defined or checked. This can be compromised by supplying data which is greater than what the entity can hold. This results in a memory spill over into other areas and thereby corrupts the instructions or code that need to be processed by the microprocessor.

When a vulnerability is exploited it results in a **security violation**, which will result in a certain **impact**. A security violation may be an unauthorized access, escalation of privileges, or denial-of-service to the IT systems.

Tools are used in the process of identifying vulnerabilities. These tools are called **vulnerability scanners**. A vulnerability scanning tool can be a hardware-based or software application.

Generally, vulnerabilities can be classified based on the **type of security error**. A type is a root cause of the vulnerability.

Vulnerabilities can be classified into the following types:

1. **Access Control Vulnerabilities**

   It is an error due to the lack of enforcement pertaining to users or functions that are permitted, or denied, access to an object or a resource.

   Examples:

   Improper or no access control list or table

   No privilege model

   Inadequate file permissions

   Improper or weak encoding

   Security violation and impact:

   Files, objects, or processes can be accessed directly without authentication or routing.

2. **Authentication Vulnerabilities**

   It is an error due to inadequate identification mechanisms so that a user or a process is not correctly identified.

   Examples:

   Weak or static passwords

   Improper or weak encoding, or weak algorithms

   Security violation and impact:

   An unauthorized, or less privileged user (for example, Guest user), or a less privileged process gains higher privileges, such as administrative or root access to the system.

3. **Boundary Condition Vulnerabilities**

   It is an error due to inadequate checking and validating mechanisms such that the length of the data is not checked or validated against the size of the data storage or resource.

   Examples:

   Buffer overflow

   Overwriting the original data in the memory

   Security violation and impact:

   Memory is overwritten with some arbitrary code so that is gains access to programs or corrupts the memory. This will ultimately crash the operating system. An unstable system due to memory corruption may be exploited to get command prompt, or shell access, by injecting an arbitrary code.

4. **Configuration Weakness Vulnerabilities**

   It is an error due to the improper configuration of system parameters, or leaving the default configuration settings as it is, which may not be secure.

   Examples:

   Default security policy configuration

   File and print access in Internet connection sharing

Security violation and impact:

Most of the default configuration settings of many software applications are published and are available in the public domain. For example, some applications come with standard default passwords. If they are not secured, they allow an attacker to compromise the system. Configuration weaknesses are also exploited to gain higher privileges resulting in privilege escalation impacts.

5. **Exception Handling Vulnerabilities**

It is an error due to improper setup or coding where the system fails to handle, or properly respond to, exceptional or unexpected data or conditions.

Example:

SQL Injection

Security violation and impact:

By injecting exceptional data, user credentials can be captured by an unauthorized entity.

6. **Input Validation Vulnerabilities**

It is an error due to a lack of verification mechanisms to validate the input data or contents.

Examples:

Directory traversal

Malformed URLs

Security violation and impact:

Due to poor input validation, access to system-privileged programs may be obtained.

7. **Randomization Vulnerabilities**

It is an error due to a mismatch in random data or random data for the process. Specifically, these vulnerabilities are predominantly related to encryption algorithms.

Examples:

Weak encryption key

Insufficient random data

Security violation and impact:

Cryptographic key can be compromised which will impact the data and access security.

8. **Resource Vulnerabilities**

It is an error due to a lack of resources availability for correct operations or processes.

Examples:

Memory getting full

CPU is completely utilized

Security violation and impact:

Due to the lack of resources the system becomes unstable or hangs. This results in a denial of services to the legitimate users.

9. **State Error**

It is an error that is a result of the lack of state maintenance due to incorrect process flows.

Examples:

Opening multiple tabs in web browsers

Security violation and impact:

There are specific security attacks, such as **Cross-site scripting (XSS)**, that will result in user-authenticated sessions being hijacked.

Information security professionals need to be aware of the processes involved in identifying system vulnerabilities. It is important to devise suitable countermeasures, in a cost effective and efficient way, to reduce the risk factor associated with the identified vulnerabilities. Some such measures are applying patches supplied by the application vendors and hardening the systems.

Penetration testing

While vulnerability assessment and remediation is used to strengthen the computer system, it is also important that suitable **penetration tests** be performed periodically to identify the possibilities of how a system may be compromised. The primary purpose of penetration testing is to identify the exploitation possibilities of an identified vulnerability.

The following diagram illustrates the process of **Vulnerability Assessment and Penetration Testing (VAPT)**:

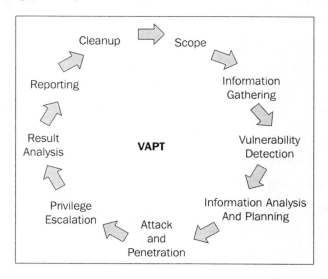

VAPT can be performed in the following nine-step process:

1. **Scope**

   While performing assessments and tests, the scope of the assignment needs to be clearly defined. The scope is based on the assets to be tested. The following are the three possible scopes that exist:

   a. **Black Box Testing**: Testing from an external network with no prior knowledge of the internal networks and systems.

   b. **Gray Box Testing**: Testing from an external or internal network, with knowledge of the internal networks and systems. This is usually a combination of black box testing and white box testing.

   c. **White Box Testing:** Performing the test from within the network with the knowledge of the network architecture and the systems. This is also referred to as internal testing.

2. **Information Gathering**

   The process of information gathering is to obtain as much information as possible about the IT environment such as networks, IP addresses, operating system version, etc. This is applicable to all the three types of scope as discussed earlier.

3. **Vulnerability Detection**

   In this process, tools such as vulnerability scanners are used, and vulnerabilities are identified in the IT environment by way of scanning.

4. **Information Analysis and Planning**

   This process is used to analyze the identified vulnerabilities, combined with the information gathered about the IT environment, to devise a plan for penetrating into the network and systems.

5. **Penetration Testing**

   In this process, the target systems are attacked and penetrated using the plan devised in the earlier process.

6. **Privilege Escalation**

   After successful penetration into the system, this process is used to identify and escalate access to gain higher privileges, such as root access or administrative access to the system.

7. **Result Analysis**

   This process is useful for performing a root cause analysis as a result of a successful compromise to the system leading to penetration, and devise suitable recommendations in order to make the system secure by plugging the holes in the system.

8. **Reporting**

   All the findings that are observed during the vulnerability assessment and penetration testing process need to be documented, along with the recommendations, in order to produce the testing report to the management for suitable actions.

9. **Cleanup**

   Vulnerability assessment and penetration testing involves compromising the system, and during the process, some of the files may be altered. This process ensures that the system is brought back to the original state, before the testing, by cleaning up (restoring) the data and files used in the target machines.

Common myths about vulnerability assessment and penetration testing

The following are some of the common myths about security assessments, such as vulnerability and penetration testing, and about information security in general:

- I use a firewall, and therefore my systems are secure
- I don't have web-based applications and am not connected to the Internet, and therefore my systems are safe
- There was no intrusion incident in the past few years, and therefore our systems are not penetrable
- I have a good security engineer, and therefore my systems are safe

Worldwide statistics of intrusions and system compromises indicate that such beliefs are not true. Proper vulnerability testing is necessary and helps in information security risk management processes.

CVE and CVSS

Many security groups, vendors, and other organizations that are involved in vulnerability research, identify vulnerabilities in the systems almost daily. There are many variations in terms of these reported vulnerabilities used by different vendors. Sometimes it is difficult to identify whether the reported vulnerability, by different vendors, is the same or different.

To address this anomaly, many of the security vendors, software vendors, and other similar business groups, formed a worldwide effort. The outcome of this group is an **online dictionary** of vulnerabilities and exposures. This online dictionary is called Common Vulnerabilities and Exposures (CVE) and is sponsored by the **Department of Homeland Security (DHS)** of USA.

CVE is an online dictionary of vulnerabilities, and there is an effort by NIST, USA as part of their **Information Security Automation Program (ISAP)** to provide **criticality rating** or **scoring** for CVE-listed vulnerabilities. This scoring is known as the Critical Vulnerability Scoring System (CVSS), and is contained in an online database known as the **National Vulnerability Database (NVD)**.

Summary

Today we focused on the vulnerability and penetration tests that give a security professional a way to identify and evaluate system weaknesses and then mitigate the risks based on the results of such tests.

We've also focused on the types of vulnerabilities, the typical security violations and their related impact on the IT systems, and also the process of conducting vulnerability and penetration tests.

Finally, we've also discussed some of the standardization efforts such as CVE and CVSS that are initiated by the standards body such as the NIST.

Tomorrow and the day after, we'll quickly review some of the important concepts in the information security domain, "cryptography".

Practice questions

1. Which of the following is not a penetration testing method?
   a) Black box testing
   b) Blue box testing
   c) Grey box testing
   d) Yellow box testing

2. Vulnerabilities in IT systems are _____.
   a) Holes or errors
   b) Software functionality
   c) Hardware functionality
   d) None of the above

3. Which of the following step is not a vulnerability assessment and penetration testing process?
   a) Scope
   b) Result Analysis
   c) Software Development
   d) Reporting

4. Common Vulnerabilities and Exposures (CVE) is a _____.
   a) Dictionary
   b) Database
   c) Software program
   d) Vulnerability

5. The National Vulnerability Database (NVD) provides _____.
   a) Common software defects
   b) Common Vulnerability Scoring System
   c) Common Vulnerability Sorting System
   d) Common hardware defects

8

Day 7: Cryptography

In the last few days, we've covered some of the important information security domains such as information security and risk management, physical security, and access control. Today and tomorrow, we'll focus on "cryptography", which not only provides data security, but also contains a myriad of concepts and techniques.

Cryptography is one of the most important domains in the CISSP examination. This domain includes important concepts which are the fundamental building blocks for information security.

Key areas of knowledge

A candidate appearing for the CISSP exam should have knowledge in the following areas in the cryptography domain. A candidate should understand:

- The application and use of cryptography
- The methods of encryption
- The types of encryption
- The initialization vectors
- The cryptographic systems
- The use of key management techniques and how to employ them
- Message digest and hashing
- The use of digital signatures
- Non-repudiation
- The methods of cryptanalytic attacks
- How to employ cryptography in network security
- The use of cryptography to maintain email security
- Public key infrastructure
- Alternatives such as steganography and watermarking

The approach

In accordance with the knowledge expected for the CISSP exam, this chapter is broadly grouped under seven sections, as shown in the following diagram:

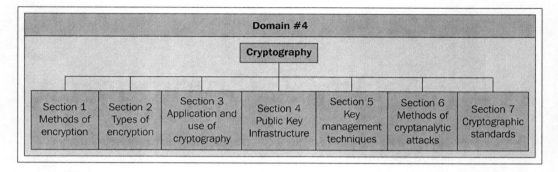

- **Section 1**: This section covers the basic concepts related to encryption and the methods of encryption.

- **Section 2**: Various types of encryption methods are used in the cryptography domain. In this section, we will be covering some of the important ones that are predominantly used, their characteristics such as the type of algorithm used, the key length, and their applications.

- **Section 3**: This section covers the application and use of cryptography in the industry.

- **Section 4**: Public Key Infrastructure (PKI) is an industry standard framework, which enables integration of various services that are related to cryptography. We'll cover, in detail, some of the important concepts in PKI.

- **Section 5**: Key management techniques are important from the perspective of cryptographic key generation including distribution to destruction. This section covers many concepts in this domain.

- **Section 6**: A cryptographic key can be compromised. The compromises can be due to a weak algorithm or weak keys. Many methods of cryptanalytic attacks exist to compromise the keys. This section covers some of the attacks that are widely used.

- **Section 7**: This section covers some of the wireless encryption standards related to cryptography. It also covers federal standard FIPS-140 that specifies security requirements for cryptographic modules.

Today we will cover some of the methods of cryptography, various types of encryption, and the application and use of cryptography.

Methods of encryption

Cryptography is an art, as well as a science, that involves the process of transforming plaintext into scrambled text and vice-versa. The purpose of cryptography is to conceal the confidential information from unauthorized eyes and ensure immediate detection of any alteration made to the concealed information.

Basic concepts

Plaintext, in the cryptographic context, is known as the **original text** that needs protection. For example, the password that you are typing is in plain text. Similarly, documents, such as business agreements and MOU, are in plain text.

Scrambled text in the cryptographic context, is known as **cipher text**. Therefore, a cipher text is the scrambled version of the plain text, which essentially means that the cipher text is not in a human-readable format.

The function of cryptography is to keep the plain text secret by scrambling it for security purposes.

The process of converting the plain text to scrambled (cipher) text is called encryption. The process of encryption is also known as **enciphering**. Hence, a cipher text can be referred to as **encrypted text**.

The process of converting scrambled (cipher) text to plain text is called **decryption**. The process of decryption is also known as **deciphering**. The output of decryption is plain text or **decrypted text**.

Encryption, as well as decryption, is based on algorithms. An algorithm in cryptography is a series of well-defined steps that define the procedure for encryption or decryption. For example, if we use a scrambling method that substitutes the alphabets by the next alphabet, than we're using a particular type of substitution algorithm. In this type of algorithm A=B, B=C....Z=A. Therefore, in this algorithm, a word such as "WELCOME" will be represented as "XFMDPNF". As you can see, this example uses only one step, but complex algorithms use multiple steps with different mathematical formulae.

 Julius Caesar used a type of shift3 cipher to communicate secret military messages. This involved substitution by 3rd alphabet.

The algorithm that is used for encryption as well as decryption is referred to as the Cipher.

A **cryptographic key**, or a **cryptovariable**, is used in the encryption and decryption of a text. This is analogous to the keys that we use in household padlocks. If you observe the physical key, you can find varying slots. These are known as tumblers or levers. By adjusting the levers, different types of key combinations are obtained. Similarly, in cryptography, we use an electronic key (cryptographic key) to lock or unlock a plain text or document, or any electronic data.

A **cryptographic method** is a way of doing encryption and decryption in a systematic way. The following diagram illustrates a cryptographic method:

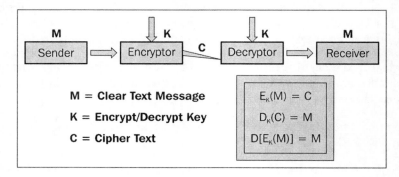

In the above process, the encrypted message of the sender is the cipher text, while the decrypted cipher text is the original message. These processes are represented as **EK(M) = C** and **DK(C)=M** respectively. Therefore, decrypting an encrypted message will result in the original message and the process can be represented as **D[EK(M)] = M**.

Types of encryption

As cryptography is based on algorithms and the keys that operate on them, types of encryption or decryption are based on these two factors (algorithms and keys). There are three types of encryption that are predominantly used in government as well as business.

Symmetric key encryption

In this type, only one key is used. The name "symmetric" implies that the key used for encryption as well as for decryption, is the same. This type of encryption is also known as **Secret Key Cryptography (SKC)**.

Symmetric key encryption is categorized into two types based on the algorithm used.

If the algorithm that is used operates on a single bit or byte, or computer word such that the key is changed constantly, it is called **stream cipher**. For example, when we want to encrypt a word such as "WELCOME" in stream cipher, each of the letters in the word will be encrypted using the algorithm. The Caesar shift3 algorithm is a stream cipher.

If the algorithm operates on a block of text, as opposed to a single bit or byte), then it is known as a **block cipher**. In this case, the algorithm will encrypt the entire word.

The following are examples of algorithms that are commonly used in the industry:

- **Stream cipher**:

    RC4 algorithm uses about 40 to 256 bits and the key sizes are different. Due to its speed, it is used in less complex hardware. Examples where RC4 is used are in protocols such as **Secure Sockets Layer** (**SSL**) and **Wireless Encryption Privacy** (**WEP**).

- **Block cipher**:

    Data Encryption Standard (**DES**) is a block cipher that uses up to 56-bit keys and operates on 64-bit blocks. It was designed by **International Business Machines** (**IBM**) and adopted by the NIST.

    Triple-DES (**3DES**), as the name implies, uses three 56-bit keys that pass over the blocks three times.

    Advanced Encryption Standard (**AES**) is a 128-bit block cipher that employs 128, 192, or 256-bit keys. This is based on the NIST specifications and is the official successor to DES.

 The present AES uses an algorithm known as **Rijndael** that uses variable block as well as key lengths.

    Blowfish is an algorithm that uses variable key lengths of 32 to 448 bits that work on 64-bit blocks.

    Twofish is a block cipher that uses 128, 192, or 256-bit keys on 128-bit blocks. This type of cipher is considered to be more secure.

    International Data Encryption Algorithm (**IDEA**) is a block cipher that uses 128-bit keys on 64-bit blocks.

A block cipher operates on different modes.

When a ciphertext block is formed by the application of secret key to encrypt the plaintext block, it is called **Electronic Code Book** (ECB).

When a plaintext is Exlusively-ORed (XORed) with the previous block of ciphertext, then the mode is called **Cipher Block Chaining** (CBC).

Cipher FeedBack (CFB) is a mode that allows the encrypted data units to be smaller than the block unit size.

Output FeedBack (OFB) uses an internal feedback mechanism so the plain text block cannot create a same ciphertext block.

Initialization vectors are a block of bits that allows either a stream cipher, or a block cipher, to execute on any of the above modes.

Asymmetric key encryption

In this type of encryption there are two keys. The name "asymmetric" implies that the keys are not the same. This type of encryption is also known as **Public Key Cryptography** (PKC).

The two keys that are used in this type are known as **private key** and **public key**. They are used in combination to encrypt and decrypt the message or text.

The following are the important concepts in PKC:

- There are two keys-private and public.
- The private key is kept secret.
- The public key is widely distributed.
- The private and public key of the entity, a person or an application software, are related by a mathematical algorithm.
- It is not possible to derive the private key from the public key.
- A message is encrypted using a recipient's public key. Hence, only the recipient's private key can be used to decrypt the message. This **ensures the confidentiality** of the message. For example, if Bob wants to send a document to Alice, then Bob will encrypt the document using Alice's public key. Therefore, Alice can open the document only by using her private key.

- **A digital signature** is a type of public key cryptography where the message is digitally signed using the sender's private key. This can be verified using the sender's public key. This is to authenticate the sender. For example, Bob will digitally sign the message that he's sending to Alice using his private key. Alice can verify the authenticity of the message by using Bob's public key.

- One of the most important purposes of public key cryptography is to ensure non-repudiation. **Non-repudiation** is a method by which neither the sender nor the receiver of the message could deny their actions.

 An asymmetric key encryption uses **one-way functions** that are easy to compute on one side and difficult to do on the other.

The following are examples of algorithms that are commonly used in the industry:

Rivest, Shamir, and **Adleman (RSA)** is an asymmetric key encryption algorithm named after its inventors. It uses a variable size encryption block as well as variable key sizes. The algorithm uses the product of two large prime numbers to derive the key-pairs.

Diffie-Hellman method is used primarily for private-key exchange over an insecure medium.

ElGamel is similar to Diffe-Hellman and is used for exchanging keys.

Elliptic Curve Cryptography (ECC) is an algorithm that generates keys from elliptical curves.

The Digital Signature Algorithm (DSA) is specified by the NIST under **Digital Signature Standard (DSS)**. This algorithm is primarily used for authentication in digital signatures.

Hashing

Hashing, or hash function, is a type of encryption where a key is not used. Instead, a hash value is computed based on the contents of the message. The computed value is known as a **checksum**. The purpose of hashing is to provide **integrity checking** to the encrypted text.

Hashing is also known as **message digest**, or **one-way encryption**, as there is no decryption, but only validating the computed checksum.

The following are examples of algorithms that are commonly used in the industry:

The Message Digest Algorithm (MD) is a series of hashing algorithms that produce 128-bit hash values from an arbitrary-length message.

The Secure Hash Algorithm (SHA) is based on the NIST's **Secure Hash Standard (SHS)**, which can produce hash values that are 224, 256, 384, or 512 bits in length.

Key length and security

In cryptography, the length of keys is not the only factor that indicates the strength or security. While a short key means less security, the same is not true for the reverse. That is, a long key does not automatically translate to strong security. The security of an encryption key lies in the quality of the encryption algorithm and entropy of the key.

Entropy of the key in cryptography means the uncertain portions of key combinations. In other words, entropy is related to randomness of the key combinations. Therefore, 1 128-bit key may not have 128-bit entropy. The greater the entropy, the stronger the key which will require more time, and computing power, to try the combinations.

Summary of encryption types

The following table summarizes the cryptographic algorithms, their key lengths, and other important details pertaining to the encryption types:

Encryption Type	Algorithm	Key Length	Application(s)
Symmetric key encryption	RC4	40 to 256 bits	Secure Sockets Layer (SSL)
			Wireless Encryption Privacy (WEP)
	Data Encryption Standard (DES)	Uses up to 56-bit keys and operates on 64-bit blocks	Secure Electronic Transaction (SET)
			Secure Sockets Layer (SSL)
			Transport Layer Security (TLS)
	Triple-DES (3DES)	Three 56-bit keys	Secure Electronic Transaction (SET)
			Secure Sockets Layer (SSL)
			Transport Layer Security (TLS)
	Advanced Encryption Standard (AES)	128, 192, or 256-bit keys	Secure Electronic Transaction (SET)
			Secure Sockets Layer (SSL)
			Transport Layer Security (TLS)
	Blowfish	32 to 448 bits that work on 64-bit blocks	Communication links
			Embedded file encryption
	Twofish	128, 192, or 256-bit keys on 128-bit blocks	Communication links
			Embedded file encryption
	International Data Encryption Algorithm (IDEA)	128-bit keys on 64-bit blocks	Pretty Good Privacy (PGP)

Encryption Type	Algorithm	Key Length	Application(s)
Asymmetric key encryption	Rivest, Shamir, and Adleman (RSA)	Variable key length	Communication links
			Embedded file encryption
	Diffie-Hellman	Variable key length	Communication links
			Embedded file encryption
	ElGamel	Variable key length	Secure Sockets layer (SSL)
	Elliptic Curve Cryptography (ECC)	Variable key length	Public Key Cryptography
			Smart cards
	Digital signature Algorithm (DSA)	Variable key length	Digital Signatures
Hashing	Message Digest Algorithm (MD)	Key not used. 128-bit hash value	For checking integrity of files such as MD5 hash
			SSL, TLS, IPSec
	Secure hash Algorithm (SHA)	Key not used. 224, 256, 384 0r 512 bit hash value	SSL, TLS, IPSec

Application and use of cryptography

Cryptographic systems are the common implementation of the standard algorithms.

The following are some of the common systems that are popular today:

- **Transport Layer Security (TLS)**, and its predecessor Secure Sockets Layer (SSL), are protocols that provide communication security by encrypting the sessions while using Internet. They use many of the cryptographic algorithms discussed above. Some of the activities that can be secured by TLS or SSL are web browsing, e-commerce transactions such as online shopping, banking, etc., and instant messaging or Internet chat.

- **Secure Electronic Transaction (SET)** is a set of standard protocols for securing credit card transactions over insecure networks. SET uses digital certificates and public key cryptography. One of the primary applications is to ensure security while using credit cards over the Internet.

- **IPsec** is a set of protocols to secure Internet communications. Authentication and encryption are the key functions. IPsec is primarily used in the implementation of **Virtual Private Networks (VPN)**.

- **Pretty Good Privacy (PGP)**, developed by Zimmermann, is a software package that supports secure email communications. Some of the security services provided by PGP include message encryption, digital signatures, data compression, and email compatibility. PGP uses IDEA for encrypting the messages and RSA for key exchanges and digital signatures.

- **Secure Multi-Purpose Internet Mail Extensions** (S/MIME) uses public key cryptography to provide authentication for email messages through digital signatures. This system uses encryption for confidentiality of the email message. This standard defines the way both parts of an email (header and body) could be constructed. This standard is also known as an extended Internet email standard as it defines the usage of multimedia content such as pictures, sound, video, etc. in email messages. MIME itself does not provide security. S/MIME is an encryption protocol that provides digital signature capabilities to email messages. Here, S denotes "secure" of .**Secure Hypertext Transfer Protocol (S-HTTP)**. This is a protocol that introduces an authentication and encryption layer between the **Hyper Text Transfer protocol (HTTP)** and Transmission Control Protocol (TCP) so as to secure the communications for the **World Wide Web (WWW)**.

- **Secure Shell (SSH)** is a protocol that establishes a secure channel between two computers for communication purposes.

- **Kerberos** is an encryption and authentication service. Kerberos is designed to authenticate network resources but does not provide third-party verification (as opposed to digital signatures). Kerberos maintains a centralized server that performs the function of key distribution and session authentication between two network resources. A single point of compromise would be the Kerberos server itself.

- **Steganography** refers to the art of concealing information within computer files such as documents, images, or any multimedia content. This is contrasted with obscuring information by encryption. Only the sender and receiver know the presence of a hidden message.

- **Digital Watermarking** is a method by which copyright information is embedded in digital content such as documents, images, and multimedia files, and so on.

- **SecureID** is a two-factor authentication system developed by Security Dynamics. A randomly generated number is used along with a PIN or password for authentication purposes. This is used in local, as well as remote, access to computers.

- **Wireless Application Protocol (WAP)** is a set of standards for wireless communications by using devices such as mobile phones. This encryption technology is used in **Wireless Transmission Layer Security (WTLS)**.

- **IEEE 802.11** is set of standards for **Wireless Local Area Networking (WLAN)**. **Wired Equivalent Privacy (WEP)** and **WI-FI Protected Access (WPA)** are the commonly used protocols for encryption in this communication standard.

Summary

Today we've covered some of the important concepts in cryptography. First, we established the methods of encryption, which in principle is enciphering and deciphering. Then we moved on to discuss different types of encryption. In essence, the encryption types are either symmetric or asymmetric. We've also covered example algorithms under each of these types.

We've dealt with public key cryptography, which is a type of asymmetric key encryption, and seen that digital signatures are its main application. We've also reviewed the function of hashing, its purpose, and the different hashing algorithms.

Finally, we've dealt with the application and use of cryptography in various day-to-day IT related activities. These activities include web browsing, email, or messaging, and also the area of wired or wireless networking.

Tomorrow we'll focus on the most important application of cryptography, which is Public Key Infrastructure. It uses the concepts of public key cryptography and key management techniques. We'll also quickly review some of the common attacks on cryptographic systems, and overview of cryptographic standards.

Practice questions

1. Which one of the following is not a type of encryption algorithm?

   a) Data Encryption Standard

   b) Advanced Encryption Standard

   c) Transport Layer Security

   d) Message Digest Algorithm

2. Symmetric Key Encryption is also known as _____.

   a) Stream cipher

   b) Block cipher

   c) Public Key Cryptography

   d) Secret Key Cryptography

3. Which one of the following is known as a cryptovariable?

   a) Plain Text

   b) Cipher Text

   c) Cipher

   d) Cryptographic Key

4. IEEE 802.11 is a set of standards for _____.

   a) Wired Local Area Networking

   b) Hyper Text Transport Protocol

   c) Secure Sockets Layer

   d) Wireless Local Area Networking

5. The primary purpose of hashing is to provide _____.

   a) Availability

   b) Integrity

   c) Confidentiality

   d) Authentication

9
Day 8: Cryptography

Yesterday we covered some of the basic concepts in the domain of cryptography. This includes elements such as encryption, decryption, the method of encryption and decryption, types of encryption such as symmetric and asymmetric, and their standard algorithms. We also focused on public key cryptography and the related concepts. We've dealt with the concepts that are related to hashing. Finally, we concluded by looking at various applications where cryptographic algorithms are implemented for security.

Today our goal is to understand more about Public Key Infrastructure (PKI) that uses the concepts of public key cryptography. Since the application of public key cryptography essentially uses asymmetric key, it is necessary to understand the importance of key management. We'll review some of the important key management techniques.

We'll move further and briefly review the various attacks on cryptographic systems, and conclude by reviewing some of the published cryptographic standards.

At the end of the day, you should be able to:

- Explain various concepts in PKI
- List various key management techniques
- Understand and explain various cryptanalytic attacks
- Understand and explain the different cryptography-related standards

Public key infrastructure

Public Key Infrastructure (PKI) is a framework that enables integration of various services that are related to cryptography.

The aim of PKI is to provide confidentiality, integrity, access control, authentication, and most importantly, non-repudiation.

Non-repudiation is a concept, or a way, to ensure that the sender or receiver of a message cannot deny either sending or receiving such a message in future. One of the important audit checks for non-repudiation is a **time stamp**. The time stamp is an audit trail that provides information of the time the message is sent by the sender and the time the message is received by the receiver.

Encryption and decryption, digital signature, and key exchange are the three primary functions of a PKI.

RSS and elliptic curve algorithms provide all of the three primary functions: encryption and decryption, digital signatures, and key exchanges. Diffie-Hellmen algorithm supports key exchanges, while **Digital Signature Standard (DSS)** is used in digital signatures.

Public Key Encryption is the encryption methodology used in PKI and was initially proposed by Diffie and Hellman in 1976. The algorithm is based on mathematical functions and uses asymmetric cryptography, that is, uses a pair of keys.

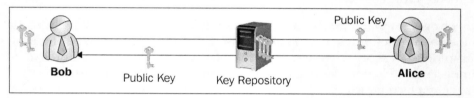

The image above represents a simple document-signing function. In PKI, every user will have two keys called a "pair of keys". One key is known as a private key and the other is known as a public key. The private key is never revealed and is kept with the owner, and the public key is accessible by every one and is stored in a key repository.

A key can be used to encrypt as well as to decrypt a message. Most importantly, a message that is encrypted with a private key can only be decrypted with a corresponding public key. Similarly, a message that is encrypted with a public key can only be decrypted with the corresponding private key.

In the example image above, Bob wants to send a confidential document to Alice electronically. Bob has four issues to address before this electronic transmission can occur:

1. Ensuring the contents of the document are encrypted such that the document is kept confidential.

2. Ensuring the document is not altered during transmission.

3. Since Alice does not know Bob, he has to somehow prove that the document is indeed sent by him.

4. Ensuring Alice receives the document and that she cannot deny receiving it in future.

PKI supports all the above four requirements with methods such as secure messaging, message digests, digital signatures, and non-repudiation services.

Secure messaging

To ensure that the document is protected from eavesdropping and not altered during the transmission, Bob will first encrypt the document using Alice's public key. This ensures two things: one, that the document is encrypted, and two, only Alice can open it as the document requires the private key of Alice to open it. To summarize, encryption is accomplished using the public key of the receiver and the receiver decrypts with his or her private key. In this method, Bob could ensure that the document is encrypted and only the intended receiver (Alice) can open it. However, Bob cannot ensure whether the contents are altered (Integrity) during transmission by document encryption alone.

Message digest

In order to ensure that the document is not altered during transmission, Bob performs a hash function on the document. The hash value is a computational value based on the contents of the document. This hash value is known as the **message digest**. By performing the same hash function on the decrypted document the message, the digest can be obtained by Alice and she can compare it with the one sent by Bob to ensure that the contents are not altered.

This process will ensure the integrity requirement.

Digital signature

In order to prove that the document is sent by Bob to Alice, Bob needs to use a digital signature. Using a **digital signature** means applying the sender's private key to the message, or document, or to the message digest. This process is known as as **signing**. Only by using the sender's public key can the message be decrypted.

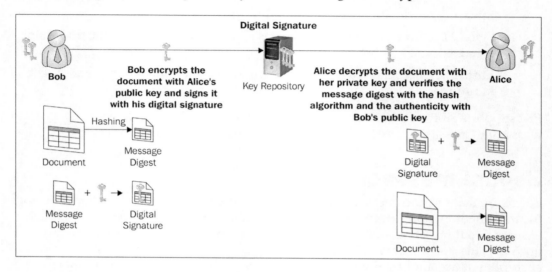

Bob will encrypt the message digest with his private key to create a digital signature. In the scenario illustrated in the image above, Bob will encrypt the document using Alice's public key and sign it using his digital signature. This ensures that Alice can verify that the document is sent by Bob, by verifying the digital signature (Bob's private key) using Bob's public key. Remember a private key and the corresponding public key are linked, albeit mathematically. Alice can also verify that the document is not altered by validating the message digest, and also can open the encrypted document using her private key.

> **Message authentication** is an authenticity verification procedure that facilitates the verification of the integrity of the message as well as the authenticity of the source from which the message is received.

Digital certificate

By digitally signing the document, Bob has assured that the document is sent by him to Alice. However, he has not yet proved that he is Bob. To prove this, Bob needs to use a digital certificate.

A **digital certificate** is an electronic identity issued to a person, system, or an organization by a competent authority after verifying the credentials of the entity. A digital certificate is a public key that is unique for each entity. A certification authority issues digital certificates.

In PKI, digital certificates are used for authenticity verification of an entity. An entity can be an individual, system, or an organization.

An organization that is involved in issuing, distributing, and revoking digital certificates is known as a **Certification Authority (CA)**. A CA acts as a notary by verifying an entity's identity.

One of the important PKI standards pertaining to digital certificates is X.509. It is a standard published by the **International Telecommunication Union (ITU)** that specifies the standard format for digital certificates.

PKI also provides **key exchange** functionality that facilitates the secure exchange of public keys such that the authenticity of the parties can be verified.

Key management procedures

Key management consists of four essential procedures concerning public and private keys. They are as follows:

1. Secure generation of keys—Ensures that private and public keys are generated in a secure manner.
2. Secure storage of keys—Ensures that keys are stored securely.
3. Secure distribution of keys—Ensures that keys are not lost or modified during distribution.
4. Secure destruction of keys—Ensures that keys are destroyed completely once the useful life of the key is over.

Type of keys

NIST Special Publication 800-57 titled "Recommendation for Key Management - Part 1: General" specifies the following nineteen types of keys.

1. Private signature key—It is a private key of public key pairs and is used to generate digital signatures. It is also used to provide authentication, integrity, and non-repudiation.
2. Public signature verification key—It is the public key of the asymmetric (public) key pair. It is used to verify the digital signature.

3. Symmetric authentication key — It is used with symmetric key algorithms to provide assurance of the integrity and source of the messages.

4. Private authentication key — It is the private key of the asymmetric (public) key pair. It is used to provide assurance of the integrity of information.

5. Public authentication key — Public key of an asymmetric (public) pair that is used to determine the integrity of information and to authenticate the identity of entities.

6. Symmetric data encryption key — It is used to apply confidentiality protection to information.

7. Symmetric key wrapping key — It is a key-encryptin key that is used to encrypt the other symmetric keys.

8. Symmetric and asymmetric random number generation keys — They are used to generate random numbers.

9. Symmetric master key — It is a master key that is used to derive other symmetric keys.

10. Private key transport key — They are the private keys of asymmetric (public) key pairs, which are used to decrypt keys that have been encrypted with the associated public key.

11. Public key transport key — They are the public keys of asymmetric (public) key pairs that are used to decrypt keys that have been encrypted with the associated public key.

12. Symmetric agreement key — It is used to establish keys such as key wrapping keys and data encryption keys using a symmetric key agreement algorithm.

13. Private static key agreement key — It is a private key of asymmetric (public) key pairs that is used to establish keys such as key wrapping keys and data encryption keys.

14. Public static key agreement key — It is a public key of asymmetric (public) key pairs that is used to establish keys such as key wrapping keys and data encryption keys.

15. Private ephemeral key agreement key — It is a private key of asymmetric (public) key pairs used only once to establish one or more keys such as key wrapping keys and data encryption keys.

16. Public ephemeral key agreement key — It is a public key of asymmetric (public) key pairs that is used in a single key establishment transaction to establish one or more keys.

17. Symmetric authorization key — This key is used to provide privileges to an entity using symmetric cryptographic method.

18. Private authorization key — It is a private key of an asymmetric (public) key pair that is used to provide privileges to an entity.

19. Public authorization key — It is a public key of an asymmetric (public) key pair that is used to verify privileges for an entity that knows the associated private authorization key.

Key management best practices

The following are some of the best practices applicable to key management:

Key Usage refers to using a for a cryptographic process, and should be limited to using a single key for only one cryptographic process. This is to ensure that the strength of the security provided by the key is not weakened.

When a specific key is authorized for use by legitimate entities for a period of time, or the effect of a specific key for a given system is for a specific period, then the time span is known as a **cryptoperiod**. The purpose of defining a cryptoperiod is to limit a successful cryptanalysis by a malicious entity.

 Cryptanalysis is the science of analyzing and deciphering codes and ciphers.

The following assurance requirements are part of the key management process:

- **Integrity protection** — Assuring the source and format of the keying material by verification

- **Domain parameter validity** — Assuring parameters used by some public key algorithms during the generation of key pairs and digital signatures, and the generation of shared secrets that are subsequently used to derive keying material

- **Public key validity** — Assuring that the public key is arithmetically correct

- **Private key possession** — Assuring that the possession of the private key is obtained before using the public key

Cryptographic algorithm and **key size selection** are the two important key management parameters that provide adequate protection to the system and the data throughout their expected lifetime.

Key states

A cryptographic key goes through different states from its generation to destruction. These states are defined as **key states**. The movement of a cryptographic key from one state to another is known as a **key transition**.

NIST SP800-57 defines the following six key states:

- Pre-activation state — The key has been generated, but not yet authorized for use
- Active state — The key may used to cryptographically protect information
- Deactivated state — The cryptoperiod of the key is expired, but the key is still needed to perform cryptographic operations
- Destroyed state — The key is destroyed
- Compromised state — The key is released or determined by an unauthorized entity
- Destroyed compromised state — The key is destroyed after a compromise or the comprise is found after the key is destroyed

Key management phases

The key states, or transitions, can be grouped under four **key management phases**. They are as follows:

- Pre-operational phase — The keying material is not yet available for normal cryptographic operations
- Operational phase — The keying material is available for normal cryptographic operations and is in use
- Post-operational phase — The keying material is no longer in use, but access to the material is possible
- Destroyed phase — The keys are no longer available

Methods of cryptanalytic attacks

Cryptanalytic attacks are keys that have been compromised by decipherment to find out the keys. The goal of cryptanalysis is to decipher the private key or secret key. The amount of information provided to the analyst, as well as the type of information provided, determines the type of attacks possible. The following are six possible attack scenarios. Candidates are advised to understand the key difference between the different types of attacks.

1. **Ciphertext only attack**: This type of attack refers to the availability of the ciphertext (encrypted text) to the cryptanalyst. With large ciphertext data, it may be possible to decipher the ciphertext by analyzing the pattern.

2. **Known-plaintext attack**: This type of attack happens when a cryptanalyst obtains a ciphertext as well as the corresponding plaintext. In this scenario, even if the data is small, it is possible to understand the algorithm.

3. **Chosen-plaintext attack**: This type of attack refers to the availability of a corresponding ciphertext to the block of plaintext chosen by the analyst.

4. **Adaptive-chosen-plaintext attack**: This type of cryptanalytic attack is known as an adaptive-chosen-plaintext attack if the cryptanalyst can choose the samples of the plaintext based on the results of previous encryptions in a dynamic passion.

5. **Chosen-ciphertext attack**: This type of attack is used to obtain the plaintext by choosing a sample of ciphertext by the cryptanalyst.

6. **Adaptive-chosen-ciphertext attack**: This type of attack is similar to the chosen-ciphertext attack, but the samples of ciphertext are dynamically selected by the cryptanalyst and the selection can be based on the previous results as well.

Cryptographic standards

Cryptography standards are related to the following:

- Encryption
- Hashing
- Digital signatures
- Public Key Infrastructure
- Wireless
- Federal standards

We've covered different cryptographic standards pertaining to encryption, hashing, digital signatures, and Public Key Infrastructure in the previous sections. In this section we'll cover the wireless standards and the Federal standard FIPS-140 for cryptographic modules.

Wireless cryptographic standards

Wireless protocols and services are predominantly governed by IEEE 802.11 standards. These standards are basically for Wireless Local Area Network (WLAN) computer communications.

The following are some of the cryptographic standards that are used in WLAN:

Wired Equivalent Privacy (WEP) is an algorithm that uses stream cipher RC4 encryption standard for confidentiality protection and CRC-32 for integrity assurance. This algorithm is now deprecated as it is easily breached.

Wi-Fi Protected Access (WPA) is a security protocol developed by the Wi-Fi alliance that replaces WEP. This protocol implements the majority of the advanced requirements in the IEEE802.11i standard released in 2004. WPA is backward compatible with WEP.

WPA2 is an advanced protocol certified by the Wi-Fi alliance. This protocol fulfills the mandatory requirements of the IEE 822.11i standard and uses the AES algorithm for encryption.

IEEE 802.11 is a set of standards that govern wireless networking transmission methods. IEEE 802.11a, IEEE 802.11b, and 802.11g are different standards based on the throughput or bandwidth and the frequency band.

IEEE 802.11i is an amendment to the original 802.11 standards.

The **Wi-Fi alliance** is a non-profit organization that supports IEEE wireless standards. The following is information about the Wi-Fi alliance as published on their web site:

"The Wi-Fi Alliance is a global, non-profit industry association of more than 300 member companies devoted to promoting the growth of (WLANs). With the aim of enhancing the user experience for wireless portable, mobile, and home entertainment devices, the Wi-Fi Alliance's testing and certification programs help ensure the interoperability of WLAN products based on the IEEE 802.11 specification."

Bluetooth is a wireless protocol for short-range communications for fixed or portable computers and mobile devices. It uses the 2.4GHz short-range radio frequency bandwidth for communication between mobile devices, computers, printers, GPS, and more. Bluetooth uses custom block ciphers for confidentiality and authentication.

Federal information processing standard

We'll cover one of the most important federal standards titled **Security Requirements for Cryptographic Modules** FIPS-140 series in the following section:

As per the published information:

The Federal Information Processing Standards Publication Series of the NIST is the official series of publications relating to standards and guidelines adopted and promulgated under the provisions of Section 111(d) of the Federal Property and Administrative Services Act of 1949 as amended by the Computer Security Act of 1987, Public Law 100-235. These mandates have given the Secretary of Commerce and NIST important responsibilities for improving the utilization and management of computer and related telecommunication systems in the Federal Government. The NIST, through its Computer Systems Laboratory, provides leadership, technical guidance, and coordination of Government efforts in the development of standards and guidelines in these areas.

The core structure of FIPS140 recommends four security levels for cryptographic modules that protect sensitive information in the federal systems. These systems include computer and telecommunication systems that include voice system as well. The levels are qualitative in the increasing order, Level 1 being the lowest and Level 4 the highest.

The following are brief descriptions of the FIPS140 levels:

1. **FIPS140 Security Level 1** — It is the basic or lowest level of security that prescribes basic security requirements for a cryptographic module, such as using at least one approved cryptographic algorithm. This level does not emphasize physical security.

2. **FIPS140 Security Level 2** — Tamper evidence mechanisms is a requirement in this level. This enhances the physical security of the device. Tamper-evident seals or coatings should be used to physically protect the device or storage that contains the cryptographic module. This level also emphasizes the implementation of role-based authentication as a minimum.

3. **FIPS140 Security Level 3** — The primary requirement is preventing an intruder from gaining access to the cryptographic modules and the **Critical Security Parameters (CSP)** contained within. This level prescribes high probability of detection and response mechanisms for physical attacks. This level emphasizes identity-based authentication.

4. **FIPS140 Security Level 4** — This is the highest level and the physical security mechanisms. A complete envelope of protection around the cryptographic module with the intent of detecting and responding to all unauthorized attempts at physical access is provided. This level requires a two-factor authentication. This level also requires the control of environmental conditions such as preventing damage to cryptographic modules due to temperature, heat, and voltage.

Summary

Today our focus was to review some of the important concepts in the PKI systems.

Cryptography relies on keys, and key management is the most important security requirement besides the strength of the algorithm. We've reviewed important concepts in this area.

We subsequently moved on to discuss some of the cryptanalytic attacks that could be perpetrated on cryptographic systems.

We've also covered the federal standard FIPS140 that prescribes security levels for cryptographic modules that protect sensitive information.

Tomorrow and the day after, we will focus on another important security domain that deals with the security requirements along with considerations that are necessary during operational aspects of systems.

Practice questions

1. Digital signature means _____.

    a) Applying sender's private key to the message

    b) Applying sender's public key to the message

    c) Applying receiver's private key to the message

    d) Applying receiver's public key to the message

2. When a specific key is authorized for use by legitimate entities for a period of time, then it is known as _____.

    a) Cryptanalysis

    b) Cryptography

    c) Cryptoperiod

    d) Key usage

3. Which one of the following is a type of cryptanalytic attack?

    a) Chosen image

    b) Chosen plaintext

    c) Adaptive image parameter

    d) Adaptive plain-ciphertext

4. Which one of the following is an application of IPSec?

    a) Wireless Application Protocol

    b) Virtual Private Networking

    c) S/MIME

    d) Social engineering

5. Steganography is a _____.

    a) Public Key Infrastructure

    b) Private Key

    c) Concealing message

    d) Watermarking

10

Day 9: Operations Security

The operations security domain is concerned with the day-to-day management of people, processes, and computer systems in order to preserve the confidentiality, integrity, and availability of information. The primary objective of operations security is to ensure correct and secure operation of information-processing facilities. Its secondary objective is to identify, implement, monitor, and manage the controls that are necessary for secure operations. Managing incidents, administrative management control, and most importantly configuration and change management form the core activities in this domain.

For the next two days, we'll focus on the important concepts and best practices followed in this domain. We'll also focus on threats and vulnerabilities that can compromise the assets which would jeopardize the operations.

Knowledge requirements

Having knowledge in the following areas that relate to operations security is essential for a candidate who appears for the CISSP exam:

- Applying various security concepts to activities
- Employee resource protection
- Incident management and reporting
- Supporting high availability
- Implementing and supporting patch and vulnerability management
- Ensuring administrative management and control
- Understanding configuration management concepts
- Responding to attacks

The approach

In keeping with the knowledge expected in the CISSP exam, this domain is broadly grouped under the following four sections:

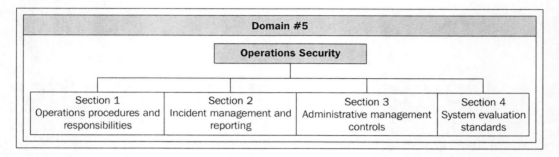

Section 1: Operations procedures and responsibilities include the procedures that are necessary for security, and the roles and responsibilities of the personnel involved in the day-to-day operations of IT systems.

Section 2: Incident management and reporting are the most important activities in the operation security domain. This section will focus on some important concepts related to them.

Section 3: Information security is about selecting and implementing suitable security controls to mitigate security risks. We will review some of the important administrative management controls in IT operations.

Section 4: IT systems need to support operations. Critical and sensitive infrastructure such as government, defense, research and development, and so on, require IT systems that satisfy certain security criteria. We will review some of the important system evaluation standards that specify such criteria.

Today we'll quickly review some of the important concepts in Sections 1 and 2.

Operations procedure and responsibilities

Operations that deal with various activities in the organization, and specifically IT operations, need to follow certain established procedures. From an operational and security perspective, these procedures are documented as IT operations that require coordinated and consistent activities. These activities are known as **documented operating procedures**.

Examples of documented operating procedures include computer start-ups and close-downs, backup of critical information, system maintenance, media handling, facility management such as computer rooms and data centers, mail management, safety procedures such as fire safety, and so on.

The International Standard ISO/IEC 27002 lists the following specific instructions that need to be available in the operating procedures:

- Processing and handling of information
- Backing up critical information
- Scheduling requirements including interdependencies with other systems, earliest job start, and latest job completion times
- Providing instructions for handling errors or other exceptional conditions which might arise during job execution, including restrictions on the use of system utilities
- Supporting contracts in the event of unexpected operational or technical difficulties
- Giving special output and media handling instructions, such as the use of special stationary or the management of confidential output, including procedures for secure disposal of output from failed jobs
- System restarting and recovery procedures for use in the event of system failure
- Managing audit trail and system log information

Operations procedures are generally considered formal documents. It is also important that specific responsibilities be established which pertain to operations as well as security.

Similarly, operations procedures must be consistent, and any changes need to be updated by the established change management procedures.

Roles and responsibilities

When we discuss operations which are specific to the IT environment, the areas of focus are the data center operations and the data processing systems. Different personnel are involved in the day-to-day operations of data centers. Some of the most important roles are system administrators, security administrators, operators, and ordinary users. Each of these personnel have different roles to play from an information security perspective. The concepts that are important from an operations security perspective are discussed next.

System administrators

An IT environment consists of both a homogeneous and heterogeneous cluster of IT systems that are housed in data centers either in a single location or distributed across different locations. A data center, and the associated IT infrastructure, consists of assets such as servers, network devices, database management systems, applications, workstations, and desktop computers.

System administrators are responsible for maintaining and monitoring these IT assets.

System administrators are also responsible for ensuring the availability of the IT assets.

Other responsibilities include maintaining the system time across all the computer systems, monitoring and troubleshooting system boot-up processes, database, network and system log maintenance, and user management in terms of creating and maintaining user accounts and passwords.

Database administrators and network administrators are two different roles that are a part of a system administrator's role. In small organizations, a single person plays these roles, and in large organizations, multiple personnel play these roles.

Security administrators

Security administration means maintaining the security aspects of IT operations. Based on the principle of "separation of duties" a security administrator should be a different person than a system administrator. However, security administrators complement the functions of the system administrators.

The role of security administrators is to provide an oversight of the security operations.

The responsibilities of security administrators include:

- Managing the security configuration settings to ensure the appropriate access controls are maintained
- Setting sensitivity labels to information for implementing and maintaining the privilege levels in access control systems
- Managing the security profiles of systems and users
- Managing and monitoring log files related to security events in order to facilitate system audits

Operators

Operators manage the day-to-day operations of the IT environment. They are entrusted with maintaining the system processes and have certain privileges pertaining to the operations.

Users

Users, sometimes referred to as ordinary users, are clients in client/server environments. They have restricted privileges and have controlled access to the system based on the sensitivity labels. The concept of "least privilege" is applicable to ordinary users.

Incident management and reporting

An incident is an event that could possibly violate information security. The violation may breach the confidentiality, integrity, and availability requirements of information assets. Primarily, incidents happen due to weaknesses in a system.

When a systematic and procedural way of managing incidents is established within an organization, it is known as **incident management**.

Incident management consists of incident reporting and responses to such reports.

Incident reporting refers to the mechanism of reporting suspected weaknesses and incidents to the management by employees, contractors, and third-party users.

Incidents

The following are examples of incidents:

- **Access violation** is a type of incident where an unauthorized entity either tries to gain access to the system or successfully gains access.

- **Malfunction of hardware and software** could possibly affect the availability of the systems. It is also possible that the data could be corrupted which would compromise integrity.

- **Human errors** such as wrong inputs to the system, improper configuration and violation of established procedures, could compromise the security.

- **Uncontrolled system changes** could affect system security in such a way that the system cannot be restored to the previous secure state or other users of the system are unaware of the changes.

- **Non-compliance with policies and procedures** is an incident that could compromise the established secure practices.

- A **physical security breach** is an incident that could compromise information security controls.

Incident management objective and goals

The objective of information security incident management is to manage incidents in an effective manner in order to mitigate risks by using timely actions.

The goal of incident management is to:

1. Establish, implement, and maintain a suitable procedure for reporting information security related incidents and weaknesses by employees, third-party contractors, and outsourced entities.

2. Establish, implement, and maintain escalation procedures related to information security incidents.

3. Establish designated points of contact for reporting information security incidents and weaknesses.

4. Periodically conduct awareness programs for the employees, third-party contractors, and outsourced service providers about information security incidents, weaknesses, and reporting procedures.

5. Ensure that the reported incidents are properly dealt with and corrective actions are taken.

6. Establish procedures to include the lessons learned from incidents within the awareness programs and management procedures.

Incident management controls

Incident management involves actions that are predominantly corrective in nature. An example of this would be fire fighting. However, certain preventive actions are taken to control the onset of an incident. Let us see some of the security controls, systems, and actions that help in incident management.

Intrusion detection system

As the name implies, **an Intrusion Detection System (IDS)** is a detective control that senses unauthorized intrusions to the premises, such as data centers or computer networks.

Vulnerability assessment and penetration testing

In physical and network security, vulnerability assessment and penetration testing are periodically conducted to identify weaknesses in the access control mechanisms, and to test the possibility of unauthorized intrusion.

Patch management

Computer applications contain vulnerabilities also known as, errors. These applications are executable files and are produced by software vendors. The vulnerabilities identified after the final release of such applications are periodically fixed by the vendors, by releasing software code containing the patches. Patch management refers to applying patches to the existing applications in a systematic way. Some of the patch management controls are applying patches to the test system before applying them to the production systems and creating a rollback mechanism if the applied patch affects the existing applications.

Configuration management

Improper configuration of IT systems will lead to an insecure system which can be compromised affecting its confidentiality and integrity. Configuration errors also affect the availability. Configuration management refers to maintaining the right configuration of the systems while documenting and managing the changes to the systems.

Business continuity planning

From an operations security perspective, business continuity planning seeks to ensure the continuity of IT operations is maintained from alternate locations during a disaster, based on the business continuity requirements. An important consideration is to maintain the security levels during such operations.

Summary

Today we covered some of the concepts and requirements in the operations security domain.

The primary requirements in this domain are procedures and responsibilities.

Threats could violate the operations security by exploiting vulnerabilities. When such an event occurs, it results in an incident. Therefore, incident management and reporting forms the core of the operations security domain.

Tomorrow we'll move on to the different controls that are necessary for ensuring secure operations and also the **Trusted Computer Security Evaluation Criteria (TCSEC)**, a requirement specified by Department of Defense.

Practice questions

1. An access violation is a(n) _____.

   a) Data Encryption Standard

   b) Procedure

   c) Incident management

   d) Incident

2. A systematic and procedural way of managing incidents is known as _____.

   a) Configuration management

   b) Incident management

   c) Change management

   d) System management

3. If an event could possibly violate information security, then such an event is known as a(n) _____.

   a) Problem

   b) Confidentiality breach

   c) Incident

   d) Integrity breach

4. Operations procedures are generally considered _____.

   a) Draft documents

   b) Draft policies

   c) Formal documents

   d) Formal records

5. Operations security is to ensure _____.

   a) Correct and secure operation of information processing facilities

   b) Correct and insecure operation of information processing facilities

   c) Incorrect and secure operation of information processing facilities

   d) Incorrect and insecure operation of information processing facilities

11

Day 10: Operations Security

Today we'll focus on the control environment to preserve the confidentiality, integrity, and availability of information assets from the perspective of administrative management of operations. We'll also review the established concepts in configuration management and their relevance in information security.

At the end of the day, you should be able to:

- Explain the concepts in administrative controls
- Understand and explain TCSEC-related concepts
- Explain the application and relevance of configuration management

Administrative management and control

Information security is effective risk management. One of the primary risk management processes is to identify the risk to information assets. The next process is known as risk assessment, which estimate the impact that the risk. Once we know the risk and its impact, the process of identifying and implementing suitable controls forms the core activity in the risk management process.

Operations, as we know, are predominantly administrative in nature. Operations security means identifying and implementing controls to mitigate security risks in operations. For example, implementing visitor access management to offices is a security control. Simple visitor access control operations require administrative tasks such as entry and exit registers. Administrative security controls for visitor access includes allowing or disallowing electronic gadgets such as camera phones, laptops, pen drives, and so on. It also includes monitoring the movement of visitors, escorting them, and gaining signatures on the visitor slip by the staff that the visitor has met.

As you can observe in this example, the controls are designed to either prevent a security breach (not allowing electronic gadgets), to detect a security breach (monitoring visitors' movements), or to correct a security breach (escorting). You'll observe that some of the controls work in more than one way. For example, escorting can be preventive (guiding a visitor through a designated path), detective (if the visitor strays from the path), and corrective as well.

The following are common terminologies related to administrative controls.

Preventive controls

An old adage says, "An ounce of prevention is worth a pound of cure." In information security, this adage is very much true. If a security breach can be prevented by some mechanism, the cost of such a mechanism is much less than fixing a breach.

Preventative controls, or **preventive controls**, are the type of controls that are preventive in nature. In other words, they act to prevent any incident of security breach. Information security risk assessments and lessons learned from incidents help in devising such controls.

The following are examples of preventive or preventative controls:

- A specific rule in a firewall that controls **Internet Control Message Protocol (ICMP)** traffic would be a preventative control. This protocol is designed to check whether a computing resource, such as a server, or a specific service is up and running. However, malicious hackers or programs may misuse it to mount the denial-of-service (DoS) attacks.

 A **ping of death**, or **ping flooding**, is a type of DoS attack that sends large, fragmented ICMP packets to the target system causing buffer overflow or sends thousands of ICMP packets to the target system affecting the normal traffic. Due to this attack, availability of the system or service will be compromised.

- The concept of least privilege is a preventative control. Controlling the resources that can be accessed by normal users and administrators prevents misuse of the resources.

 The principle of **least privilege** is to provide only those privileges to the users that are necessary for operations. User access control in modern operating systems is an example of such a principle.

Detective controls

A risk is a perception. There is a common saying in the security domain that it is practically impossible to provide 100% security, or achieve 0% risk, using security controls. A residual risk will remain even after implementing controls. Therefore, deploying a completely effective preventive control is not possible.

When a preventive security control is breached, or there is a security breach due to lack of security controls, there should be a mechanism to identify these breaches. Detective controls are designed to identify security breaches and, as the name implies, detect events after their occurrence.

The following are examples of detective controls:

- An Intrusion Detection System that detects the presence of an intruder in the network is an example of this control.

> Intrusion detection is useful to identify unauthorized access to the network or applications. While Intrusion Detection Systems (IDS) are detective controls, Intrusion Protection Systems (IPS) act as preventive controls.

- Any monitoring activity is a detective control, which includes log monitoring, parsing exceptional events in financial transactions, and so on. In the financial domain, activities such as budget and transaction monitoring, audit trails, accountability, and reconciliation of accounts are detective controls.

Corrective controls

When security breachs occur, merely detecting them in real time or later may not be sufficient to control their impact. For example, a virus outbreak in a network should be controlled before it spreads to other networks. Therefore, the affected network should be isolated to prevent the spread of the virus. **Reactive controls**, or **corrective controls**, are controls that react to a security breach.

The following are examples of corrective or reactive controls:

- An alert system is a reactive control that alerts the relevant personnel upon detection of a security breach. A duress alarm used in ATMs of banks is a reactive or corrective control.

A **duress alarm** is a system that alerts, and takes some specific actions, when invoked by an event or a user. In some countries, banks issue a duress pin number to users. In an emergency (for example, if a user is forced to withdraw money from an ATM by a robber), instead of entering the normal pin, this duress pin may be used. The functions of duress alarms are to alert the nearest branch, and in some cases the police, and disburse some small amount of money to prevent suspicion.

- Mantrap systems in data centers are reactive controls.

A **mantrap space**, or a **dead space**, is an area between two doors. In such systems, one door must close before the other opens. In the event of intrusion alarm, the system reacts by locking all the doors and trapping the intruder.

Other controls

There are many other controls that are not purely preventive, detective, or corrective in nature. Based on the application or usage, controls can also be a combination of the three primary administrative controls.

Recovery controls

Recovery controls are generally restorative controls that restore the systems back to their normal operations.

For example, a Disaster Recovery Process is a recovery control.

Deterrent controls

Deterrent controls deter a person, or a process, from attempting a security breach.

For example, guards and dogs are deterrent controls.

Compensating controls

Compensating controls, as the name implies, compensates for a lack of control by other means.

For example, a patch may not be available for a known vulnerability. In such a case, a compensating control will monitor the vulnerable application or port.

System controls

Computer systems also require other controls for proper operations. The following are some examples of such controls.

An **application control** is a control mechanism built into software applications to prevent, detect, or react to an event such as access or modification to the application. The purpose of an application control is to ensure complete and accurate processing of data and preserving confidentiality, integrity, and availability of applications of the data they process. Also, application controls maintain the privacy requirements of data and control the input and output processes.

The following are common areas where application control mechanisms are used:

- Completeness: Ensures that the data is complete and accurate
- Validation: Checks whether the data is correct
- Identification: Identifies the correct resources
- Authentication: Authenticates the correct resources
- Authorization: Maintains access controls to the resources

Input and **output controls** ensure security while providing input to the systems or applications, and the information that is being sent out.

A popular attack on database systems using SQL is known as an **SQL Injection**. In such an attack, malformed data is provided to the input query to the database. If the input validation mechanisms are weak in such systems, the attack can compromise the database, affecting the confidentiality and integrity of the data.

Transaction controls are used to introduce checks and balances in the transaction system such that the security is not breached. **Processing controls** are designed to ensure secure processing of the information. The applications, data, or system does not remain constant. Frequent changes occur in the information processing systems. **Change controls** ensure security during such changes to systems.

Computer systems, be it software or hardware, need to be tested before being deployed in a production environment. Changes to the system also require testing processes. A **test control** ensures that the systems are tested for security assurance requirements before being deployed.

System evaluation standards

From the operations security perspective, the following standards are important in the security evaluation of systems.

Trusted Computer System Evaluation Criteria (TCSEC)

The TCSEC is a United States **Department of Defense (DOD)** standard for computer system security. This standard defines criteria for assessing effectiveness of controls built into computer systems.

 The United States government, between 1980 and the 1990s, published a series of standards pertaining to computer security. This series of standards is published using different colors for the cover page. This color coding is popularly known as the **Rainbow Series** or **Rainbow Books**.

The TCSEC was published in an orange-colored cover and is popularly known as the **Orange Book**.

The TCSEC has four fundamental objectives or requirements. They are policy, accountability, assurance, and documentation.

The Orange Book (TCSEC) mandates two types of assurance requirements for trusted computers: operational assurance and life cycle assurance.

Operational assurance consists of system architecture, system integrity, covert channel analysis, trusted facility management, and trusted recovery.

Life cycle assurance consists of security testing, design specification and testing, configuration management, and trusted distribution.

The separation of users and data is an example of operational assurance, while configuration management is an example for life cycle assurance.

The TCSEC defines four divisions in the scale of lowest to highest security. The levels C, B, and A have subdivisions. The main division and their corresponding subdivisions are as follows:

D—Minimal protection

C—Discretionary protection

- C1—Discretionary Security Protection
- C2—Controlled Access Protection

B — Mandatory protection

- B1 — Labeled Security Protection
- B2 — Structured Protection
- B3 — Security Domains

A — Verified protection

- A1 — Verified Design

Based on the TCSEC, the following controls need special attention. Their division is shown in brackets:

Separation of users and data (C1) refers to access control mechanisms that prevent accidental deletion of data between users. Similarly, **separation of duty** refers to mechanisms of distribution of duties between two different entities (entity predominantly refers to different personnel) for ensuring security. For example, system administration and security administration are two different duties that need to be separated.

Audit trails (C2) are primarily documentary evidence that relate to transactions. They are a traceback mechanism that aids in identifying various events such as date and time of a transaction, the entity (normally a person) that processed the transaction, the computer system or terminal from which the transaction was processed, and other details such as security events. All these events are recorded or logged in an **audit log**.

Covert channels (B2 and B3) are secret or hidden channels that transmit information to unauthorized entities. These channels draw information from authorized channels without the knowledge of the user. **Covert timing channel** refers to the manipulation of resources based on the response time of the system. **Covert storage channel** refers to the modification of stored data to convey information to other programs or processes. **Steganography** is a type of covert channel that hides information behind an image. One of the main threats is steganography, which can be used by terrorists and international criminals to hide and transmit data.

Configuration management (B2) refers to managing configuration changes to systems such as hardware and software or data and information, in a systematic way to avoid and detect any unauthorized modifications. Controls are placed in the system which pertain to configuration changes, so as to preserve security. These are known as **change controls**.

Trusted Computing Base (TCB) (A1) refers to the entire computing system of hardware and networks, including the associated components, such as software, that are critical, and security protection in its entirety. In other words, a security event may compromise the entire system.

Common Criteria (CC)

The **Common Criteria for Information Technology Security Evaluation** (CC) is an information security standard that ensures the following:

- Products can be evaluated by competent and independently licensed laboratories in order to determine the fulfillment of particular security properties, to a certain extent or assurance

- Supporting documents are used within the Common Criteria certification process to define how the criteria and evaluation methods are applied when certifying specific technologies

- The certification of security properties for an evaluated product can be issued by a number of Certificate Authorizing Schemes, with this certification being based on the result of their evaluation

CC is adapted as an ISO standard and is published as ISO/IEC 15048. CC is covered in detail on Day 16 in the chapter *Security Architecture and Design*.

Summary

Today our focus was on controls. In the operations security domain, controls are prominently administrative in nature. The aim is to ensure security by preserving the confidentiality, integrity, and availability of information assets during their day-to-day operations.

Operations controls are preventive, detective, and reactive in nature. Other technical controls, such as input and output, or processing and transaction controls, ensure security to the information while being accessed or processed.

The TCSEC is an evaluation criterion for US defense systems to assure security. Its primary aim is to assess the effectiveness of controls that are built into the systems.

We'll discuss "Application Security" tomorrow and the day after, and review some of its important concepts.

Practice questions

1. Preventive controls are not used to _____.

    a) Prevent a security event

    b) Set up a rule in firewall such that malicious traffic is filtered

    c) Identify intrusion detection

    d) Identify a virus

2. Compensating controls are _____.

    a) Preventive controls

    b) Detective controls

    c) Recovery controls

    d) Alternative controls

3. Which one of the following is not a B1 type of objective in Trusted Computing Security Evaluation Criteria?

    a) Discretionary security protection

    b) Labeled security protection

    c) Verified design

    d) Separation of users and data

4. Covert channels are _____.

    a) Security feature

    b) Secret channel

    c) Authorized Channels

    d) Access control mechanism

5. Configuration management is to manage _____.

    a) Configuration changes

    b) Covert channel

    c) Trusted Computing Base

    d) Uncontrolled changes

12

Day 11: Application Security

Applications are one of the most important building blocks of the IT infrastructure. Applications provide a way to achieve tasks that are related to the input, processing, and output of data. Also, they are used to store, retrieve, process, transmit, and destroy data. Therefore, it is of great importance to ensure the security of applications. A primary area that security professionals should focus on during the design stage of the application is security requirements. An application contains software code, and it is important that secure coding practices are used throughout the **Software Development Life Cycle (SDLC)**.

Knowledge requirements

Related to application security, the following areas should be well understood by a candidate appearing for the CISSP exam:

- The role of security in the system life cycle
- The application environment and security controls
- Databases and data warehousing, and protect against vulnerabilities and threats
- Applications and system development knowledge as well as security-based systems such as expert systems
- Applications, system vulnerabilities, and threats
- Application security-related controls

The approach

On the basis of knowledge that's expected for the CISSP exam, this domain is broadly grouped into five sections as shown here:

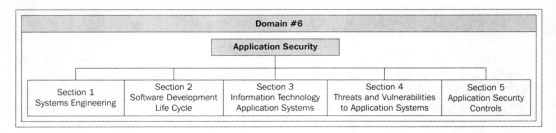

Section 1: Systems engineering concepts relate to the application of engineering concepts to the system development life cycle. Security considerations during the development cycle will reduce the number of vulnerabilities in the final products.

Section 2: Software development life cycle implies the processes that are involved during the development of a software application. Different security controls, as well as testing, are required at each stage of development to ensure fewer vulnerabilities in the final products.

Section 3: Information technology application systems consist of object-oriented systems, expert systems, database systems, and so on. Each of these application systems has unique applications and usage. Security in such systems is of great importance.

Section 4: Application development processes are not robust enough to identify and isolate all vulnerabilities at the development stage. Also, the heterogeneous nature of IT environment aggravates the security issue. This section discusses the common threats and vulnerabilities to application systems.

Section 5: Application security controls are necessary to protect the applications from compromise so that the confidentiality, integrity, and availability of information is preserved. This section discusses some of the important security controls.

Today we'll focus on Sections 1 and 2.

Systems engineering

Systems engineering is a term that implies the application of engineering concepts along with designing application systems that are complex and large.

A system may be defined as a combination of elements or parts that work together to produce an output or achieve an objective. In a system, the parts or elements are interrelated.

There are many organizations in the world that publish standards, models and principles, and practices pertaining to systems engineering. One of them is the **International Council on Systems Engineering (INCOSE)**. It is a not-for-profit membership organization founded to develop and disseminate the interdisciplinary principles and practices that enable systems to be successfully created. The **Software Engineering Institute (SEI)** at Carnegie Mellon University develops and maintains a **Capability Maturity Model (CMM)** pertaining to software development process maturity.

According to INCOSE, "Systems Engineering is an interdisciplinary approach and means to enable the realization of successful systems. It focuses on defining customer needs and required functionality early in the development cycle, documenting requirements, then proceeding with design synthesis and system validation while considering the complete problem."

System Development Life Cycle

System development follows a cyclic approach. When a system is developed using the system engineering processes, the development activities go through a specific life cycle model that is known as the **System Development Life Cycle (SDLC)**.

A life cycle model consists of many processes from establishing the needs (initiation) to archival or destruction (disposal).

System development phases

The NIST special publication 800-14 titled *Generally Accepted Principles and Practices for Securing Information Technology (IT) Systems* defines five phases in the system development life cycle. The following diagram illustrates them:

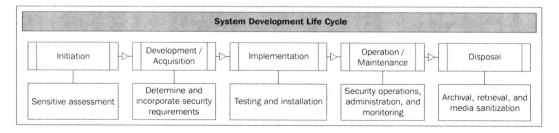

The **Initiation phase** establishes the need for the system and creation of the associated documentation. A requirement at this phase is for conducting a **sensitivity assessment**. The scope of the assessment is to look at the sensitivity of the information to be processed as well as the sensitivity of the system.

The second phase is the **Development/Acquisition phase**. In this phase, the system is designed, purchased, programmed, developed, or otherwise constructed. This phase requires the following three activities to be performed:

- Determining the security requirements
- Incorporating the security requirements into specifications
- Obtaining the system and related security activities

The third phase is the **Implementation phase**. This phase emphasizes testing and installation of the systems. The primary requirements are installing and turning on controls so that security features are enabled and configured. Performing security testing is also a requirement that includes the following:

- Testing of particular parts of the system that have been developed or acquired
- Testing the entire system
- Obtain system security accreditation

The fourth phase is the **Operation/Maintenance phase** in which the system performs its work and is continuously modified. The security considerations in this phase are related to security operations and administration, operational assurance, audit, and monitoring.

The final phase is the **Disposal phase**, which involves disposition of information, hardware, and software. The security considerations in this phase are related to archiving and retrieval as well media sanitization.

Software Development Life Cycle

Developing software systems goes through many processes. The activity or cycle starts from specification development where the overall system is designed and implemented.

Based on the system design, software programs are written, the system is documented, and operating procedures are written.

During the entire process of the software development life cycle, other activities are involved to ensure functionality of the developed application. Verification and validation are two important activities during development and implementation.

Verification is an activity that establishes the adherence to software specifications, while **validation** establishes fitness to the system in keeping with the design and requirements.

Many life cycle models are used in software development. The objectives of such models are to develop quality software applications or products that meet specifications, customer requirements, and are financially viable in terms of budgets and timelines.We'll now look at some of the models used in software development.

The **Simplistic model** is one that takes the approach of sequential stages in software development. In this model, the concept of rework does not arise and it is assumed that each stage of development is finalized before moving to the next stage.

The **Waterfall model** is a type of simplistic model where development flows like water falling from top to bottom through a series of steps. This model assumes that activities such as requirements analysis, design, implementation, testing, integration, and maintenance are completed in sequence. This model's top-down approach will have difficulty when the system design or software application has to be reworked.

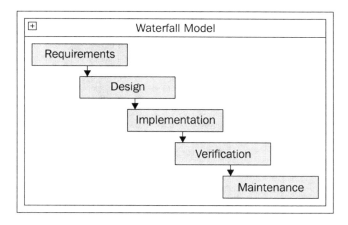

Iterative models use the concepts of iterative processes during software development. In other words, there is an element of rework allowed to improve the systems.

Incremental models allow development in terms of parallel development and are developed at different times and integrated all together.

The **Spiral model** is a type of iterative model. This model specifies the design and prototyping stages. This model proposes top-down as well as bottom-up approaches so that rework is possible. This model was defined by Barry Boehm and can be seen in the following figure:

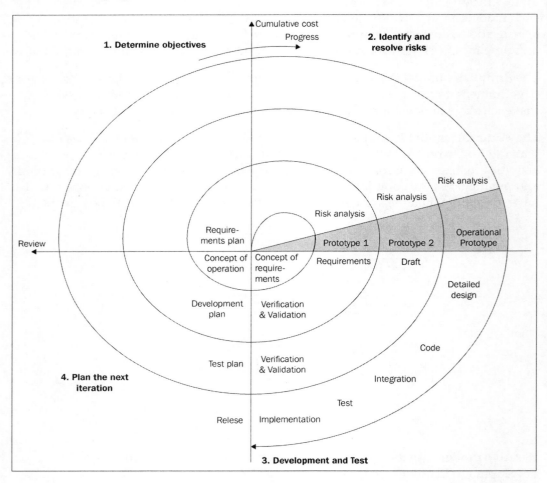

The **Agile framework** emphasizes the concept of iterations throughout the software development life cycle.

Security standards for software development processes

Security standards that focus on application security specify the standardized processes and best practices for secure software development. We've covered some of the popular SDLC models that focus on functionality or quality aspects of the applications. However, due to the numerous identified security breaches of applications, many international organizations have come out with security models and standards that are necessary to produce secure applications. Let us review some of the prominent standards.

The core security considerations that need to be applied in all standards can be grouped into the following areas, which will be covered in the book:

- User authentication
- Password management
- Access controls
- Input validation
- Exception handling
- Secure data storage and transmission
- Logging
- Monitoring and alerting
- System hardening
- Change management
- Application development
- Security assessments and audits

Systems Security Engineering—Capability Maturity Model (SSE-CMM)

An engineering model describing the essential characteristics of an organization's secure engineering practices was published by Carnegie Mellon University (CMU) titled SSE-CMM. This model addresses security engineering activities that span the entire trusted product or secure system life cycle. These activities include concept definition, requirements analysis, design, development, integration, installation, operations, maintenance, and decommissioning.

SSE-CMM divides secure system development processes in two broad categories. These categories are:

- Project and organization processes: Organization-specific processes during system and software development
- Security engineering processes: Processes that should adhere to security engineering practices during system and software development

This model is now adopted by the ISO committee and is published as ISO/IEC 21827. The following diagram from the SSE-CMM website depicts various processes in this model:

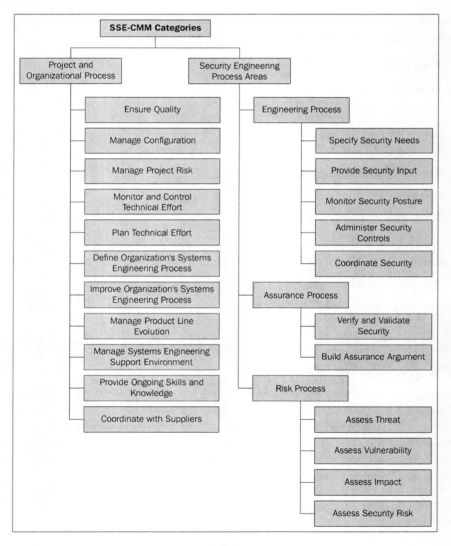

ISO/IEC 27002

International standard "ISO/IEC 27002—Code of practice for information security management" suggests some of the best practices that should be followed during system and software development.

The following are some of the best practices:

- Specifying security controls while developing new systems is enhancing the existing systems

- Validating input data, controlling internal processing, ensuring message integrity, and validating output data

- Protecting confidentiality, authenticity, and integrity of information that is being processed by the applications

- Controlling operational software, protecting system test data, and controlling access to program source code

- Changing control procedures to assist in securing development and support processes

- Testing vulnerabilities during system development, change, or enhancement

Summary

Today we covered some of the concepts in the areas of software engineering, System Development Life Cycle, and Software Development Life Cycle.

In summary, software engineering is an engineering discipline that is concerned with the process of achieving a common goal or reaching a common objective by different entities that are interrelated.

System Development Life Cycle (SDLC) is a concept of a development process from initiation to disposal.

There are many Software Development Life Cycle models based on top-down and bottom-up approaches. Also, these models are iterative and incremental in nature.

Tomorrow we will quickly review different IT systems that are commonly used, threats and vulnerabilities to application systems, and application control concepts.

Practice questions

1. According to the International Council on System Engineering (INCOSE), the focus of system engineering is NOT on _____.

   a) Defining customer needs early in the development cycle

   b) Defining functionality early in the development cycle

   c) Defining functionality in the later stages of development

   d) Documenting requirements

2. According to NIST 800-14, incorporating security requirements into specifications is a requirement in the _____.

   a) Initiation phase

   b) Implementation phase

   c) Disposal phase

   d) Development/acquisition phase

3. Waterfall model is NOT a(n) _____.

   a) Top-down model

   b) Bottom-up model

   c) Incremental, bottom-up model

   d) Iterative, top-down model

4. The spiral model specifies _____.

   a) Design and development

   b) Design and drawing

   c) Design and prototyping

   d) Development

5. In the System Development Life Cycle (SDLC), verification and validation are used for _____.

   a) Establishing fitness to the system in keeping with the design and requirements, and establishing adherence to software specifications respectively

   b) Establishing adherence to software specifications and establishing fitness to the system according the design and requirements respectively

   c) Establishing logical access to the system as per the design and requirements ,and establishing the verification to software specifications respectively

   d) Establishing software specifications, and establishing adherence to hardware specifications respectively

13

Day 12: Application Security

Today we will focus on application security including threats, vulnerabilities, and so on, and application controls in IT systems that are used in organizations to support business needs. As a security professional, you should be able to understand the functions of application systems and take into consideration the security controls available in them. It is also important that security requirements are considered and addressed during an application's design stage to minimize the vulnerabilities in the final product. "Security by design" should be the mantra for robust and secure applications. To that effect, knowing the vulnerabilities and attack points in the existing system would help in avoiding them during new application development and enhancing the applications that are being used.

At the end of the day, you should understand and be able to explain:

- Various types of IT systems
- Various threats and vulnerabilities
- Various attacks on application systems
- Various types of application control mechanisms

Introduction to Information Technology systems

Information technology systems can be broadly classified as:

- Object-oriented systems
- Artificial intelligence systems
- Database systems

These systems may be centralized or decentralized in the sense that they are distributed.

Object-oriented systems

Object-oriented systems use the concept of "objects." Objects work together with other objects in a system to achieve certain functionalities and objectives. Since related and common tasks are grouped together as an object, these systems are considered more reliable and less prone to security issues that are a result of changes in the software code.

Object-oriented programming (OOP)

Object-oriented programming uses a collection of objects that communicate and coordinate with other objects to achieve a desired functionality or an objective. The functions of the objects include sending or receiving messages, and processing instructions.

Some of the fundamental concepts that are used in object-oriented programming are as follows:

Class: It defines the characteristics and behaviors of an object.

Object: It is a pattern, example, or model of a class.

Instance: When a class creates a specific object during runtime, it is known as an instance of that class.

Method: It is an ability of an object.

Message passing: It is a communication process to invoke a method by one object to another.

Inheritance: Classes have subclasses. These subclasses inherit any characteristics of the main class.

Encapsulation: It is a wrapper. It can conceal the functional details of an object to the class.

Abstraction: It is the simplification of a complex structure through the use of modeling.

Polymorphism: It is the process of treating derived class members just like their parent-class members.

Object-Oriented Analysis (OOA): It is an analysis process for producing a conceptual model.

Object-Oriented Design (OOD): It is used to design the ways to implement the conceptual model produced in the analysis process.

Artificial Intelligence (AI) systems

It is the science and engineering of making intelligent systems that can perceive the immediate environment and take appropriate action, which maximizes its chances of success.

AI systems, which are used in information technology, try to mimic human brains in perception and decision-making. From the security perspective, an AI system can be a protector from, and perpetrator of, attacks.

An **expert system** is a system based on artificial intelligence that tries to reproduce the performance of one or more human experts.

A **neural network** is a type of artificial intelligence system that tries to mimic the neural processing of human brain. It is used in applications such as speech recognition, image analysis, software agents, and so on.

Database systems

A database system defines the storage and manipulation of data. A **Database Management System (DBMS)** is a set of software programs that is used to perform and control the operations of a database system.

A DBMS consists of a modeling language, data structures, database query language, and transaction mechanisms.

Threats and vulnerabilities to application systems

A security professional must focus on the following when considering security to applications.

Asset: An asset is basically a resource. It may be a computer, an operating system, a DBMS, and so on. In the application security parlance, an asset is the application itself.

Threat: A threat is an entity or event that could compromise an asset by exploiting any weaknesses or vulnerabilities in the asset. Some common threats to the applications are malware such as viruses, worms, trojan horses, logic bombs, and so on.

Threat agent: A threat cannot manifest on its own. It needs an agent to exploit vulnerabilities. For example, fire is a threat and not having a fire extinguisher is vulnerability. Fire needs a combustible material to spread, which is actually a threat agent. Similarly, a malicious hacker is a threat agent for unethical hacking.

Vulnerability: It is a weakness in the system that a threat could exploit. Having poor or substandard non-fireproof cabling in a data center is a vulnerability, which could be prone to short circuit or burning due to fire. Examples of application vulnerabilities include access control weaknesses, authentication errors, insufficient boundary checking, and so on. We've covered these vulnerabilities in *Chapters 6* and *7* titled *Access Control*.

Attack: It is a technique used by a threat agent to exploit vulnerabilities. For example, a malicious hacker may inject malformed data in a web application to exploit a weakness and gain access. Examples of attacks include the man-in-the-middle attack, session hijacking, buffer overflow attacks, and so on. We've covered these attacks in the *Chapters 6* and *7*, *Access Control*.

Countermeasure: These are preventative, corrective, or reactive steps to a vulnerability or an attack. The countermeasures are security controls that we are covering throughout this book.

Application vulnerabilities

Vulnerabilities in applications are based on the functionality weaknesses, a weakness that manifests in the application due to a security flaw. We've seen earlier that vulnerabilities in applications are due to improper design, improper coding, or a combination of both.

Due to an increased exploitation of applications by malicious entities and an incessant failure of applications (such as frequent crashing of applications), it has become imperative that application security is addressed for safer computing. There are many governmental organizations and security groups across the world who continually work on standardizing vulnerability classifications. One such effort by the US government is the **National Vulnerability Database (NVD)**. This database contains the enumeration of common vulnerabilities grouped as the **Common Weakness Enumeration (CWE)**. Another important project is the **Open Web Application Security Project (OWASP)** by a volunteer-based group. This project focuses on application security vulnerabilities that are specific to web applications.

[The web links or URLs are provided in the References section of this book.]

Common weakness enumeration

According to the NVD:

The Common Weakness Enumeration Specification (CWE) provides a common language of discourse for discussing, finding and dealing with the causes of software security vulnerabilities as they are found in code, design, or system architecture. Each individual CWE represents a single vulnerability type.

The vulnerability types in the CWE are as follows:

- Authentication Issues: Failure to properly authenticate users.
- Credentials Management: Failure to properly create, store, transmit, or protect passwords and other credentials.
- Permissions, Privileges, and Access Control: Failure to enforce permissions, or other access restrictions for resources, or a privilege management problem.
- Buffer Error: Buffer overflows and other buffer boundary errors in which a program attempts to put more data in a buffer than the buffer can hold, or when a program attempts to put data in a memory area outside of the boundaries of the buffer.
- Cross-site request forgery (CSRF): Failure to verify that the sender of a web request actually intended to do so. CSRF attacks can be launched by sending a formatted request to a victim, then tricking the victim into loading the request (often automatically), which makes it appear that the request came from the victim. CSRF is often associated with Cross-Site Scripting (XSS), but it is a distinct issue.
- Cross-site scripting (XSS): Failure of a site to validate, filter, or encode user input before returning it to another user's web client.
- Cryptographic Issues: An insecure algorithm, or the inappropriate use of one; an incorrect implementation of an algorithm that reduces security; the lack of encryption (plaintext); also, weak key or certificate management, key disclosure, random number generator problems.
- Path Traversal: When user-supplied input can contain ".." or similar characters that are passed through to file access APIs, causing access to files outside of an intended subdirectory.
- Code Injection: Causing a system to read an attacker-controlled file and execute arbitrary code within that file. Includes PHP remote file inclusion, uploading of files with executable extensions, insertion of code into executable files, and others.
- Format String Vulnerability: The use of attacker-controlled input as the format string parameter in certain functions.
- Configuration: A general configuration problem that is not associated with passwords or permissions.

- Information Leak, or Disclosure: Exposure of system information, sensitive or private information, fingerprinting, and so on.

- Input Validation: Failure to ensure that input contains well-formed, valid data that conforms to the application's specifications. Note: this overlaps other categories like XSS, Numeric Errors, and SQL Injection.

- Numeric Errors: Integer overflow, signedness, truncation, underflow, and other errors that can occur when handling numbers.

- OS Command Injections: Allowing user-controlled input to be injected into command lines that are created to invoke other programs, using system() or similar functions.

- Race Conditions: The state of a resource can change between the time the resource is checked to when it is accessed.

- Resource Management Errors: The software allows attackers to consume excess resources, such as memory exhaustion from memory leaks, CPU consumption from infinite loops, disk space consumption, etc.

- SQL Injection: When user input can be embedded into SQL statements without proper filtering or quoting, leading to modification of query logic or execution of SQL commands.

- Link Following: Failure to protect against the use of symbolic or hard links that can point to files that are not intended to be accessed by the application.

- Design Error: A vulnerability is characterized as a "design error" if there no errors exist in the implementation or configuration of a system, but the initial design causes a vulnerability to exist.

Web application security

Web applications are becoming popular and are increasingly being used by government, universities, and business organizations. The convenience of delivering services, such as banking, ecommerce, egovernance, and education, from a centralized location to users around the world is taking this technology to dizzying heights. However, the **World Wide Web (WWW)** or Internet is an open network that can be accessed by anyone using a connected computer. Also, due to the myriad of programming languages and systems used by different organizations, there are innumerable security threats and vulnerabilities to web applications.

The Open Web Application Security Project (OWASP) is a volunteer-based project that lists the common threats, attacks, and vulnerabilities to web applications. The OWASP groups and classifies viruses, worms, Trojan horses, and logic bombs as non-target specific threat agents.

Common web application vulnerabilities

The following is a review of some of the unique web application vulnerabilities:

- Code Permission: It refers to weaknesses in access control restrictions to the code and methods.

- Code Quality issues: It involves poor quality of code such as erroneous string compare, unused methods, misspelled method names, or leftover debug code in the applications.

- Protocol Errors: It means omitting certain important check values in the protocol such as checksums.

- Session Management: It is related to weaknesses in the applications that allow session compromises such as session hijacking.

- Synchronization and Timing Vulnerability: It is similar to race conditions in CWE, where the state of a resource can change between the time the resource is checked to when it is accessed.

- Unsafe Mobile Code: Mobile code is executed in the target user's machine. Any weaknesses in such code can be used to compromise the target machine.

- Use of Dangerous API: The Application Programming Interfaces (API) are sets of functions that can be called from an application program to access features of another program. If the called program has vulnerabilities, the calling application will also become vulnerable to attacks.

Common web application attacks

- Abuse of functionality: It means the normal functionality of an application is abused to compromise the security. For example, it is normal for web browsers to cache web pages. This functionality reduces the number of fetch attempts to the server and delivers the frequently visited web pages faster. An attack known as **cache poisoning** tries to abuse this functionality. For example, if the cache information on a proxy server is poisoned, or loaded with malicious code, then all users accessing the web site through that proxy server will be inadvertently downloading malicious content to their machines or will be redirected to illegitimate web sites.

- Data structure attacks: These types of attacks tend to alter the data in the primary memory (RAM) either by overflow, or by rearranging the order of execution or malicious code execution through data buffer. For buffer overflow errors, refer to *Chapter 7, Access Control*.

- Exploitation of authentication: This is accomplished through bypassing authentication mechanisms or controlling the actions of an authenticated user. The CSRF explained in CWE is an example of such an attack.

- Injection: It means injecting malicious or unformatted data, queries, or instructions into the application. SQL injection is an example of such an attack.

- Embedded malicious code: Malicious code is embedded in the applications. Logic bombs and Trojan horses are examples of such code.

- Path traversal attack: These attacks exploit path vulnerabilities to access the files and folders that are not intended to be accessed.

- Probabilistic techniques: These are attacks that use various combinations to guess credentials or capture keys. Examples are brute forcing of passwords or cryptanalysis.

- Protocol manipulation: It involves exploiting the features and weaknesses in the protocols. For example, data from an untrusted source enters the web server using an HTTP protocol request.

- Resource depletion: Consuming the memory, network, or disk resources. Denial-of-Service (DoS) is an example of such an attack.

- Resource manipulation: It means compromising an application by manipulating the resources. For example, a repudiation attack manipulates the logging mechanisms such that the audit trail can be defeated.

- Sniffing attacks: These attacks capture the network traffic to glean confidential information. **Evesdropping** is an example of such an attack

- Spoofing: Such attacks intercept the communication between computers or applications and impersonate them. The Man-in-the-middle attack is an example of spoofing.

Application controls

Application controls are mechanisms to preserve the confidentiality, integrity, and availability of application systems and the data they process, store, or transmit.

The following are some important controls in this domain:

Memory and address protection is a control to ensure controlled access to the memory and address locations by the application. The core focus is to limit access and prevent overwriting other memory areas.

Access control is a process to ensure access to authorized entities while blocking unauthorized entities.

File protection is a mechanism to ensure that files are accessed and modified by authorized entities in a controlled manner.

Authentication is a process to identify and authorize legitimate entities.

Reliability is a quality parameter to assure that the application systems perform efficiently and effectively.

Summary

Today our focus was on IT systems, the threats and attacks that could exploit vulnerabilities in the application systems, and application controls. Our aim is to ensure security by preserving the confidentiality, integrity, and availability of IT systems and applications from intentional or unintentional malicious operations.

We also reviewed some of the common vulnerabilities and attacks to web applications. Due to their open nature, web applications are prone to many attacks and a security professional should be cautious while designing such applications.

We'll move on to telecommunication and network security tomorrow and discuss some important concepts in that area.

Practice questions

1. An expert system tries to reproduce _____.

   a) Performance of human experts

   b) Human intelligence

   c) Characteristics of humans

   d) Physical characteristics of humans

2. Polymorphism in object-oriented systems is _____.

   a) Equating an object with the class

   b) A method of communication between objects

   c) Treating derived class members just like their parent class members

   d) A wrapper

3. Memory and address protection is _____.

   a) Physical access to a computer

   b) Controlling access by applications or entities

   c) A type of backup

   d) None of the above

4. An attack is a _____.

   a) Vulnerability

   b) Threat

   c) Technique

   d) Compromise

5. Encapsulation is a _____.

   a) Wrapper

   b) Threat

   c) Software application

   d) Class

14

Day 13: Telecommunications and Network Security

The telecommunication and network security domain deals with the security of voice and data communications through local area, wide area, and remote access networking. The focus is to understand the networking models such as **Open Systems Interconnect (OSI)** and TCP/IP models, as well as the security mechanisms for Internet, Intranet, and Extranet in terms of firewalls, routers, and intrusion detection and protection systems. CISSP candidates are expected to have knowledge in the areas of securing communication, securing networks, threats, vulnerabilities, and attacks. They should also be well informed about attack countermeasures to communication networks and protocols that are used for remote access.

Today and tomorrow we'll focus on areas pertaining to telecommunications and network security, and the necessary controls to ensure confidentiality, integrity, and availability of network communications.

Knowledge requirements

Any candidate appearing for the CISSP exam should be acquainted with areas related to telecommunications and network security, as mentioned here. The candidate should understand:

- The network architecture, protocols, and technologies
- The Open Systems Interconnect model (OSI)
- The Transmission Control Protocol / Internet Protocol (TCP/IP) model
- The application of most widely used protocols in the TCP/IP model
- The threats, vulnerabilities, and countermeasures in this domain

The approach

On the basis of knowledge that's expected in the CISSP exam, this domain is broadly grouped under one master category and four subcategories, as shown in the following diagram:

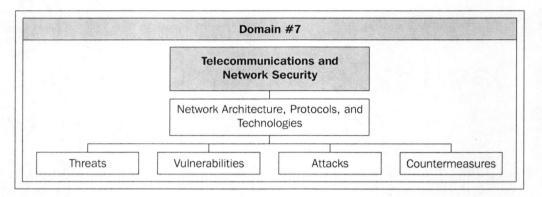

Network architecture, protocols, and technologies section covers the Open System Interconnect (OSI) and TCP/IP model in detail. In today's sections, we'll cover layered security architecture, the OSI model, and the TCP/IP model. We will look at important protocols in the application layer of the TCP/IP protocol suit including applications, threats, vulnerabilities, and countermeasures.

In the next chapter, we'll discuss the other layers of the TCP/IP protocol suit, some of the important telecommunication technologies, and the underlying security concepts.

Network architecture, protocols, and technologies

Communication is the process of transmitting information from one entity (sender) to another entity (receiver) through the use of a medium. The information may be in a written format, a spoken language, or in a sign language. The medium can be physical, such as a sender using post card to send information to receiver. The post card is transported physically by post offices. The medium can be the atmosphere as in spoken conversations.

Telecommunication, in similar terms, transmits information from entities such as people, phones, or computers to entities such as people, phones, or computers. The medium used in telecommunications is either cables or wires, or the atmosphere as in wireless connections.

In physical communications, when two people want to converse, there is a common language known to each person. Telecommunications uses an analogous system known as protocols. Also, when systems are used to communicate information, they are networked using certain binding technologies.

We have seen that information security is compromised when a threat exploits vulnerabilities in the systems. In the telecommunication domain we have many common threats that could exploit certain common and unique vulnerabilities. We will discuss some of the common countermeasures, or risk mitigation techniques, for such security exploitations.

For the convenience of grouping and greater assimilation, this chapter is organized based on the layers of network architecture. Threats, vulnerabilities, exploits, and countermeasures are provided under each protocol or the technology.

Let us review the fundamentals of network architecture in a telecommunication environment, the protocols, and the technologies used in the following sections.

Layered architecture

Layered architecture is a technique that is used to design communication networking in the form of layers. Each layer is independent, and communicates with its immediate upper and lower layers. This technique allows isolation of network components without affecting the components in other layers.

Open Systems Interconnect (OSI) Model

Open Systems Interconnect (OSI) is a layered architecture standard that defines a framework for implementing protocols in seven layers. The OSI framework architecture was developed by The International Organization for Standardization (ISO).

 A **protocol** is a communication standard that defines the rules pertaining to syntax, semantics, and synchronization for communications.

The seven layers of the OSI model are shown in the following figure:

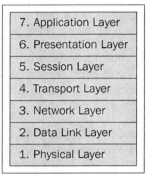

| 7. Application Layer |
| 6. Presentation Layer |
| 5. Session Layer |
| 4. Transport Layer |
| 3. Network Layer |
| 2. Data Link Layer |
| 1. Physical Layer |

Layers 7, 6, 5, and 4 work at the host (computer) level and are sometimes known as **host layers**. Layers 3, 2, and 1 are related transmissions through the media and are known as **media layers**.

Layer	Function
Layer 7: Application Layer	Provides application services that are required for application processes
Layer 6: Presentation Layer	Manages the way in which information or data is encoded or represented
Layer 5: Session Layer	Manages communication between two computers
Layer 4: Transport Layer	Maintains the integrity and validity of the data being transported
Layer 3: Network Layer	Ensures that proper route is established for transporting the data
Layer 2: Data link Layer	Ensures the node-to-node validity of the data being transmitted
Layer 1: Physical Layer	Deals with the electrical and mechanical characteristics of the data

OSI mnemonics are used to remember the order of the seven layers of the OSI model. The following are a couple of the most popular OSI mnemonics:

- All People Seem To Need Data Processing
- Please Do Not Take Sales People's Advice

OSI by illustration

Observe the following illustration and you'll find that the communication between two computers is affected as communication passes between the different layers. The top four layers communicate through the protocol stack, while the bottom three layers are routed by networking devices.

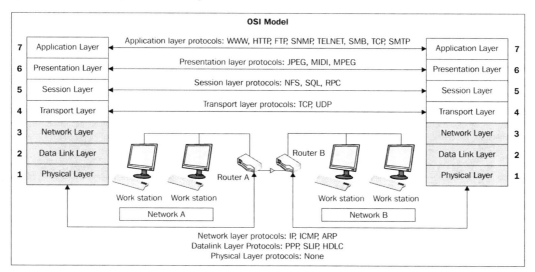

Transmission Control Protocol/Internet Protocol (TCP/IP)

TCP/IP is an Internet protocol suit on which most of the Internet and commercial networks run. This suit is named after the two important protocols—TCP and IP.

The original TCP/IP reference model consisted of four layers that are purely related to Internet communications. The four layers are **Application Layer, Transport Layer, Network/Internet Layer**, and **Data Link Layer**. The fifth layer was added in the five-layered model to represent the **Physical Layer**.

The following diagram illustrates the five-layered TCP/IP model:

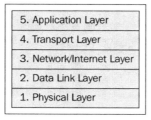

TCP/IP Protocols

TCP/IP has many defined protocols working in different layers. We will review some of the important protocols in the sections that follow.

Application layer protocols

Domain Name System (DNS)

DNS works at the application layer that translates domain names to IP addresses. This helps routers to route the traffic to the correct resource. The following table illustrates the applications, threats, vulnerabilities, attacks, and countermeasures to DNS protocols and services:

Protocol / Service	Domain Name System (DNS)
Layer(s)	DNS works in the application layer of TCP/IP model.
Applications	The main purpose of DNS is to resolve host names to the matching numeric IP addresses.
	The other applications include maintaining resource records for email and other services so that the end-to-end delivery is assured.
Threats	Spoofing
	Cache Poisoning
Vulnerabilities	Misconfigured DNS servers
Attacks	Spoofing
	DNS Cache Poisoning
Countermeasures	Domain Name System Security Extensions (DNSSEC)

Spoofing is a term that is used in computer security for the successful masquerading of one entity as another. An entity can be a person or a program. Masquerading refers to disguising, impersonating, or masking. In the context of DNS, a spoofing attack would divert the traffic to an illegitimate IP address or a site, usually attacker-constructed sites, as DNS is used to resolve host names to IP addresses.

Many spoofing attacks exist. Examples include:

- **Man-in-the-middle attack**: This attack refers to spoofing the systems, primarily, to listen to network traffic between two entities and to capture data packets. This is done to gain access to all the messages and the systems.
- **URL spoofing**: Uniform Resource Locator (URL) is a method by which a web page or a web site is identified by the browser. This is also known as website address or webpage address. By spoofing the URL, a web browser is led to believe that it is accessing the requested legitimate web site while it is not. Phishing is one such attack that uses this spoofing technique.

- **Phishing**: A spoofing technique used by fraudsters to capture sensitive information such as usernames, password, credit card details, and so on. While URL spoofing is used to redirect a user to an attacker-constructed illegitimate web site, email spoofing is used to lure the user to open an illegitimate spoofed URL.

- **Email spoofing**: This is a technique to masquerade a legitimate source, such as banks, of the email. Due to this, a user is led to believe that an email is from a trusted source.

- **SMS spoofing**: It is similar to email spoofing; but in this case, the mobile number of the source is masqueraded by a malicious entity to send a spoofed message.

Cache poisoning: This attack is used for corrupting the cache data held by browsers, devices, and applications. **DNS Cache Poisoning** deals with altering the DNS cache data with illegitimate entries. Since DNS resolves the IP addresses, poisoned data would redirect a legitimate address request to an illegitimate address.

Domain Name System Security Extensions (DNSSEC): The DNSSEC is a set of extensions that provide origin authentication, data integrity, and authenticated denial of existence. The primary purpose of DNSSEC is to prevent **Zone Enumeration**.

Zone Enumeration: It is the practice of discovering the full content of a zone via successive queries. Zone enumeration was non-trivial prior to the introduction of DNSSEC, according to RFC5155 - DNS Security (DNSSEC) Hashed Authenticated Denial of Existence.

Dynamic Host Control Protocol (DHCP)

In an Internet Protocol (IP) network, client devices obtain necessary network parameters from a centralized server(s) using this protocol. One of the primary parameters obtained is the IP address. DHCP helps reducing manual configurations.

Protocol / Service	Dynamic Host Control Protocol (DHCP)
Layer(s)	DHCP works in the application layer of the TCP/IP model.
Applications	DHCP is primarily used for assigning IP addresses to servers and clients. This protocol also uses **Point-to-Point Protocol** (PPP) and **Network Address Translation** (NAT) for assigning IP addresses to on-demand hosts, such as dialup and broadband.
	DHCP is generally not used for routers and firewalls.
	The IP address allocation is either automatic or manual, depending on the level of user intervention required. The address allocation method used is known as Request, Offer, Send, and Accept (ROSA).

Protocol / Service	Dynamic Host Control Protocol (DHCP)
Threats	Cache Poisoning
	Masquerading
Vulnerabilities	Misconfigured DHCP and DNS servers.
	Lack of session authentication and encryption.
Attacks	Birthday attack and DNS Forgery
Countermeasures	Transport Layer Security (TLS)
	Secure Sockets Layer (SSL) and Secure Shell (SSH)
	Digital signatures

Masquarading is a type of attack wherein an attacker, or a process, masks itself as a legitimate user or process to deceive an application or user. Trojan Horses are a type of malware that masquerades as a useful program.

Birthday attack is a cryptographic attack to guess a random input data. It works on a mathematical probability theory that there is a chance that more than 50% of the randomly chosen people in a group of 23 may have the same birthday. The probability increases to 99% when the group is of more than 57 people.

DNS Forgery is a type of DNS cache poisoning wherein DNS data is forged with illegitimate entries.

Transport Layer Security (TLS) and **Secure Sockets Layer** (SSL) are cryptographic protocols. The purpose of these protocols is to provide secure communication by the way of encryption.

Secure Shell (SSH) is a network protocol that facilitates secure encrypted communications between two computers.

Digital Signature is a type of public key cryptography where the message is digitally signed using the sender's private key. The purpose is to authenticate the sender.

Hyper Text Transfer Protocol (HTTP)

Internet web pages on the World Wide Web (WWW) are coded in the Hyper Text Markup Language (HTML). The HTTP is a communication protocol that enables retrieval and transfer of hypertext pages.

The HTTP uses Transmission Control Protocol (TCP) for connections.

Protocol / Service	Hyper Text Transfer Protocol (HTTP)
Layer(s)	HTTP works in the application layer of the TCP/IP model.
Applications	HTTP is the default protocol for serving web pages. Hence, this protocol is the primary delivery mechanism for web pages.
Threats	Spoofing
	Unauthorized disclosure
	Path traversal
Vulnerabilities	Weaknesses in coding header information.
	Weak encoding of get methods
Attacks	DNS spoofing
	Denial of service
	Eavesdropping
Countermeasures	Using strict validation
	Using HTTPS protocol for transmission of sensitive information

Path traversal relates to unauthorized access to the web server directory structure. Generally, the server should return an HTTP web page.

Eavesdropping is a type of attack used to listen to the communication between a client and a server in a surreptitious manner.

Validation is one of the important web based activities. For example, when a form is submitted through a web page, a **strict validation** ensures that malicious code is not inserted through forms into the receiving application.

Secure Hyper Text Transfer Protocol (S-HTTP or HTTPS) uses **Secure Sockets Layer (SSL)** for encrypting the session between the server and the client.

File Transfer Protocol (FTP) and TELNET

FTP is a network protocol that is used for transferring files from one computer to another over a TCP/IP network.

TELNET stands for TELecommunication NETwork, and is used for logging into remote servers over TCP/IP.

Protocol / Service	File Transfer Protocol (FTP) and TELNET
Layer(s)	FTP and TELNET work in the application layer of the TCP/IP model.
Applications	The main application of FTP is to transfer files between computers. FTP is not suitable for executing programs in the target servers.
	The purpose of TELNET is to log into the remote server and to perform maintenance work in that system from a remote location.
Threats	Data Capture
	Password Capture
Vulnerabilities	Passwords are in clear text
	Data transmission is in clear text (except for binary files).
Attacks	Eavesdropping
	Sniffing
Countermeasures	Secure File Transfer Protocol (SFTP)
	Secure Shell (SSH)

Sniffing is used to capture data that flows through the network and analyze it to obtain sensitive information.

Secure File Transfer Protocol (SFTP) uses SSL for transmitting files and session data. This ensures that the session is encrypted end-to-end.

Post Office Protocol 3 (POP3) and Internet Message Access Protocol (IMAP)

POP3 and IMAP protocols are used to retrieve emails from email servers over a TCP/IP connection.

Protocol / Service	Post Office Protocol 3 (POP3) and Internet Message Access Protocol (IMAP)
Layer(s)	POP3 and IMAP work in the application layer of the TCP/IP model.
Applications	The POP3 protocol is used by email clients to download email messages from the remote email server. Unless configured, this protocol is designed to delete the mails after download.
	IMAP is used to view email messages in the server. Unless offline mode is enabled, the messages are not stored in the local machine and those in the server are not deleted.

Protocol / Service	Post Office Protocol 3 (POP3) and Internet Message Access Protocol (IMAP)
Threats	Non-delivery of emails
	Unsolicited Commercial Email
Vulnerabilities	Misconfigured email servers
Attacks	Email relay
	Spoofing
Countermeasures	Strong authentication
	Source verification

Unsolicited Commercial Email (UCE) is also known as **spam**. Due to vulnerabilities in the **Mail Transport Agents (MTA)**, a commercial mail that is spam is relayed to many email accounts.

Simple Network Management Protocol (SNMP)

As the name implies, this network protocol is used for managing administrative tasks in the network.

Protocol / Service	Simple Network Management Protocol (SNMP)
Layer(s)	SNMP works in the application layer of the TCP/IP model
Applications	Managing uptime of the network, network query, measuring throughput are some of the primary applications
Threats	Unauthorized data capture
	Sensitive information disclosure
Vulnerabilities	Misconfigured servers
	Default community strings
Attacks	Packet sniffing
	Brute force and dictionary attacks
	IP Spoofing
Countermeasures	Strong passwords
	Proper configuration

Brute force and dictionary attacks use a combination of words in dictionary, along with numeric and special characters, to crack the encrypted password hashes.

Transports Layer Security (TLS) and Secure Sockets Layer (SSL)

The TLS ensures the confidentiality and integrity of data while it is transmitted.

SSL is a predecessor to TLS.

Protocol / Service	Transport Layer Security (TLS) and Secure Sockets Layer (SSL)
Layer(s)	TLS and SSL work in the application layer of the TCP/IP model
Applications	Encrypt the sessions and transport data.
	Both these protocols are cryptographic protocols
Threats	Unauthorized information access
Vulnerabilities	Software vulnerabilities
Attacks	Replay attacks
Countermeasures	Strong validation of the session data

Replay attacks refer to the gaining of attacks by capturing and replaying the session data to the application. If a vulnerability exists in handling the session data, then unauthorized access can be gained to the application system.

Summary

Today we have covered some of the concepts in the telecommunications and network security domain.

We've reviewed the Open System Interconnect (OSI) and the TCP/IP protocol suit. It is important to remember that there are many incomplete specifications. The TCP/IP model is the basis on which the Internet and many commercial networks work.

Tomorrow we'll review the remaining four layers: Transport layer, Network/ Internet layer, Data link layer, and Physical layer in the five-layered TCP/IP model. We'll also cover some telecommunication technologies and their underlying security concepts.

Practice questions

1. A protocol is a _____.

    a) Data Encryption Standard

    b) Layered architecture

    c) Communication standard

    d) Data link

2. Spoofing is a type of _____.

    a) Vulnerability

    b) Masquerading

    c) Protocol

    d) Layer in a TCP/IP model

3. An attack is a _____.

    a) Threat

    b) Vulnerability

    c) Technique

    d) Protocol

4. Transport Layer Security and Secure Sockets Layer are/do NOT _____.

    a) Protocols

    b) Use cryptographic algorithms

    c) Vulnerabilities

    d) Use encryption

5. Replay attacks are used to _____.

    a) Gain unauthorized access to the application systems

    b) Resolve domain names

    c) Break cryptographic keys

    d) Set up secure connections

15

Day 14: Telecommunications and Network Security

The telecommunications and network security domain consists of networking models that are made of many protocols. OSI and TCP/IP are the most important models that follow a layered approach to networking. Yesterday we covered some of the important concepts in these two models. From the security perspective, we've covered important application layer protocols, their applications, threats, vulnerabilities, attacks, and countermeasures in the TCP/IP suit. Today we'll focus on other protocols that constitute the TCP/IP layers. We'll also discuss some of the communication technologies at the end of this chapter to conclude our discussion of the domain.

At the end of the day, you should understand and be able to explain the following topics:

- Different protocols that are in transport layer, network/internet layer, and link layer in the TCP/IP model
- Some threats and vulnerabilities that are prevalent to such protocols
- Common attacks and possible countermeasures
- Important technologies and the security issues associated with them

Transport layer

- The transport layer in the TCP/IP model does two things: it packages the data given out by applications to a format that is suitable for transport over the network, and it unpacks the data received from the network to a format suitable for applications.

- The process of packaging the data packets received from the applications is known as **encapsulation**. The output of such a process is known as **datagram**.

- Similarly, the process of unpacking the datagram received from the network is known as **abstraction**.

A transport section in a protocol stack carries the information that is in the form of datagrams, Frames and Bits.

Transport layer protocols

There are many transport layer protocols that carry the transport layer functions. The most important ones are:

- Transmission Control Protocol (TCP): It is a core Internet protocol that provides reliable delivery mechanisms over the Internet. TCP is a connection-oriented protocol.

- User Datagram Protocol (UDP): This protocol is similar to TCP, but is connectionless.

A **connection-oriented protocol** is a protocol that guarantees delivery of datagram (packets) to the destination application by way of a suitable mechanism. For example, a three-way handshake syn, syn-ack, ack in TCP. The reliability of datagram delivery of such protocol is high.

A protocol that does not guarantee the delivery of datagram, or packets, to the destination is known as **connectionless protocol**. These protocols use only one-way communication. The speed of the datagram's delivery by such protocols is high.

Other transport layer protocols are as follows:

- **Sequenced Packet eXchange (SPX)**: SPX is a part of the IPX/SPX protocol suit and used in Novell NetWare operating system. While Internetwork Packet eXchange (IPX) is a network layer protocol, SPX is a transport layer protocol.

- **Stream Control Transmission Protocol (SCTP)**: It is a connection-oriented protocol similar to TCP, but provides facilities such as multi-streaming and multi-homing for better performance and redundancy. It is used in Unix-like operating systems.

- **Appletalk Transaction Protocol (ATP)**: It is a proprietary protocol developed for Apple Macintosh computers.

- **Datagram Congestion Control Protocol (DCCP)**: As the name implies, it is a transport layer protocol used for congestion control. Applications include Internet telephony and video or audio streaming over the network.

- **Fiber Channel Protocol (FCP)**: This protocol is used in high-speed networking such as Gigabit networking. One of its prominent applications is **Storage Area Network (SAN)**.

 SAN is network architecture that's used for attaching remote storage devices such as tape drives, disk arrays, and so on to the local server. This facilitates the use of storage devices as if they were local devices.

Let us review the most important protocols — TCP and UDP — in the following sections.

Transmission Control Protocol (TCP)

TCP is a connection-oriented protocol that is widely used in Internet communications. As the name implies, a protocol has two primary functions. The primary function of TCP is the transmission of datagram between applications, while the secondary function is related to controls that are necessary for ensuring reliable transmissions.

Protocol / Service	Transmission Control Protocol (TCP)
Layer(s)	TCP works in the transport layer of the TCP/IP model
Applications	Applications where the delivery needs to be assured such as email, World Wide Web (WWW), and file transfers, use TCP for transmission
Threats	Service disruption
Vulnerabilities	Half-open connections
Attacks	Denial-of-service attacks such as TCP SYN attacks
	Connection hijacking such as IP Spoofing attacks
Countermeasures	Syn cookies
	Cryptographic solutions

A half-open connection is a vulnerability in TCP implementation. As discussed earlier, TCP uses a three-way handshake to establish or terminate connections. Refer to the following illustration:

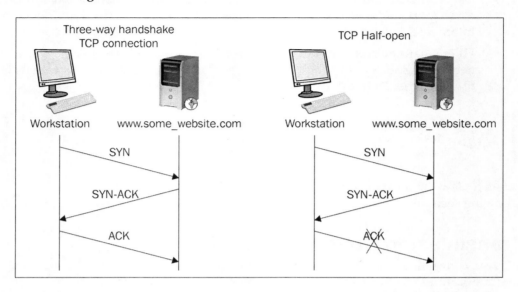

In a three-way handshake, first the client (workstation) sends a request to the server (`www.some_website.com`). This is known as an SYN request. The server acknowledges the request by sending SYN-ACK and, in the process, creates a buffer for that connection. The client does a final acknowledgement by sending ACK. TCP requires this setup because the protocol needs to ensure the reliability of packet delivery.

If the client does not send the final ACK, then the connection is known as **half-open**. Since the server has created a buffer for that connection, certain amounts of memory or server resources are consumed. If thousands of such half-open connections are created maliciously, the server resources may be completely consumed resulting in a denial-of-service to legitimate requests.

TCP **SYN attacks** are technically establishing thousands of half-open connections to consume the server resources. Two actions can be taken by an attacker. The attacker, or malicious software, will send thousands of SYN to the server and withhold the ACK. This is known as **SYN flooding**. Depending on the capacity of the network bandwidth and the server resources, in a span of time the entire resources will be consumed. This will result in a denial-of-service. If the source IP were blocked by some means, then the attacker, or the malicious software, would try to spoof the source IP addresses to continue the attack. This is known as **SYN spoofing**.

SYN attacks, such as SYN flooding and SYN spoofing, can be controlled using **SYN cookies** with cryptographic hash functions. In this method, the server does not create the connection at the SYN-ACK stage. The server creates a cookie with the computed hash of the source IP address, source port, destination IP, destination port, and some random values based on an algorithm, which it sends as SYN-ACK. When the server receives an ACK, it checks the details and creates the connection.

A **cookie** is a piece of information, usually in a form of text file, sent by the server to client. Cookies are generally stored on a client's computer and are used for purposes such as authentication, session tracking, and management.

User Datagram Protocol (UDP)

UDP is a connectionless protocol similar to TCP. However, UDP does not provide delivery guarantee of data packets.

Protocol / Service	User Datagram Protocol (UDP)
Layer(s)	UDP works in the transport layer of the TCP/IP model
Applications	UDP is predominantly used where a loss of intermittent packets is acceptable, such as video or audio streaming
Threats	Service disruptions
Vulnerabilities	Weak validation
Attacks	UDP flood attacks such as ping of death
Countermeasures	Controlling ICMP access

Ping of death refers to sending a large number of ICMP packets to the server in order to crash the system.

Pinging is a process of sending Internet Control Message Protocol (ICMP) ECHO_REQUEST message to servers or hosts to check whether they are up and running. As the process implies, a server or host on network responds to a ping request which is known as **echo**.

Network or Internet layer

The Network or Internet layer in the TCP/IP model is for internetworking. This layer has a group of methods, functions, and protocols to facilitate communication between different networks. The communication between networks is achieved through a mechanism known as **gateways**.

Network/Internet layer protocols

The protocols in this layer primarily carry out the following functions:

- They pass the outgoing packets to the next layer (datalink) through the gateway
- They pass the incoming packets to the transport layer
- They provide error detection and diagnostics for the incoming and outgoing packets

Some of the important protocols in this layer are Internet Protocol (IP), Internet Communication Message Protocol (ICMP), Internet Group Management Protocol (IGMP), and Internet Protocol security (IPsec).

The ICMP is used for error and diagnostic functions, and IGMP is used in multicasting.

 Multicasting refers to one-to-many communications. For example, a stock exchange may require sending stock price data to multiple groups or an IPTV to multicast to many users at once.

We'll review some of the important concepts in the Internet Protocol (IP) that are used for packet transmission and IPsec. They provide authentication and encryption services to the IP packets.

Internet Protocol (IP)

A connectionless protocol that is used in packet-switched networks such as the Internet. The primary function of this protocol is to send data from one computer to other.

Protocol / Service	Internet Protocol (IP)
Layer(s)	The IP works in the Network Layer of OSI and Internet layer of the TCP/IP model.
Applications	The primary application is to send data packets across the network to the destination computer. The computers in such a network are known as hosts. IP is a connectionless protocol that tries the best effort method delivery of packets, but does not guarantee it. The Transmission Control Protocol (TCP) manages the reliability of the transmission.
	Two versions are being used on the Internet: Internet Protocol version 4 (IPv4), and Internet Protocol version 6 (IPv6).

Protocol / Service	Internet Protocol (IP)
Threats	Mis-delivery or non-delivery of packets
	Data corruption
	Duplicate data
Vulnerabilities	Lack of validation
	Lack of sequencing
Attacks	Identity theft
	Hacking
Countermeasures	Transmission Control Protocol (TCP) and Address Resolution Protocol (ARP)
	IPv6 and IPSec

Internet Protocol version 4 (IPv4) is a widely deployed protocol on the Internet. As the name implies, it is the fourth iteration of the protocol. It uses 32 bits for the length of the address and its maximum limit is up to 232 addresses. The number of publicly available IPv4 addresses is more or less consumed, and the Internet is moving towards IPv6.

Internet Protocol version 6 (IPv6) is designed as a successor to IPv4 address spaces. This protocol uses 128 bits for IP addresses and has an address space of 2128 IP addresses.

IPsec protocols

IPsec is a suit of protocols that is created to secure Internet Protocols (IP). It provides authentication and encryption functions. Compared to the upper-layer security protocols such as SSL or TLS, IPsec is independent of applications. It can be used to protect the application and transport layer protocols.

IPsec uses the following three protocols for various security functions:

- **Internet Key Exchange (IKE)**: It is used to negotiate protocols and algorithms, and also to generate keys for encryption and authentication
- **Authentication Header (AH)**: It is used to provide data origin authentication to datagrams and integrity assurance
- **Encapsulation Security Payload (ESP)**: It is used to support encryption-only and authentication-only configurations

Protocol / Service	IPsec
Layer(s)	IPsec works in the network layer of the OSI and the Internet layer of the TCP/IP model
Applications	The primary functions include authentication and encryption
	This protocol suit is designed to protect transport layer protocols such as the TCP and UDP
	A Virtual Private Network (VPN) is one of the key applications of the IPsec
Threats	Spoofing
	Unauthorized connections
Vulnerabilities	Weak authentication
	Lack of connection checks
Attacks	Man-in-the-middle attacks
	Session hijacking
Countermeasures	Proper IPsec policies
	Additional IPsec connection checks

A **Virtual Private Network (VPN)** is a virtual network that is set up to use larger public network such as the Internet. The VPN uses a concept known as "tunneling" to route the data and the IPsec protocols used for end-to-end encryption.

 A **tunnel** in a computer network, such as the VPN, is a secure path or route for the datagram to pass through an insecure or un-trusted network. Protocols such as the IPsec, the **Point-to-Point Tunneling Protocol (PPTP)**, and **Layer 2 Tunneling Protocol (L2TP)** are some example of tunneling protocols.

Link layer

The methods, protocols, and specifications that are used to link hosts, or nodes, in a network are grouped as a link layer. A link layer operates close to physical layer components.

Link layer protocols

The following protocols operate on the link layer:

- **Address Resolution Protocol (ARP)**: It is used for resolving hardware address for a given IP address

- **Reverse Address Resolution Protocol (RARP)**: It is used to obtain IP addresses based on hardware address

- **Neighbor Discovery Protocol (NDP)**: It is used to find neighbor nodes in an IPv6 network

Address Resolution Protocol (ARP)

This protocol is a standard method for finding hardware addresses from network layer addresses such as the Internet Protocol (IP).

Protocol / Service	Address Resolution Protocol (ARP)
Layer(s)	The ARP works in the network layer of the OSI and the link layer of the TCP/IP model.
Applications	The primary application of the ARP is to translate IP addresses to Ethernet Media Access Control (MAC) addresses.
	The primary purpose of this protocol is to resolve hardware addresses such that communication can be established between two computers within the same network or over the Internet.
Threats	Sniffing
	Spoofing
Vulnerabilities	Unsolicited ARP reply
Attacks	ARP poisoning
	ARP Poison Routing (APR)
	Denial-of-service (DOS)
Countermeasures	MAC to IP mapping

ARP poisoning refers to overwriting existing entries in the ARP table with malicious addresses.

Media Access Control (MAC) is a unique hardware address that is assigned to the **Network Interface Cards (NIC)** or the Network Adapters.

Border Gateway Protocol (BGP)

This protocol is a type of "routing protocol" that is used in the Internet. The primary purpose is to decentralize Internet routing.

Protocol / Service	Border Gateway Protocol (BGP)
Layer(s)	The BGP works in the network or data link layer of the TCP/IP model
Applications	Internet Service Providers (ISP) predominantly use this protocol for routing the data and information between them
Threats	Mis-delivery or non-delivery of packets
	Misuse of network resources
	Network congestion
	Packet delays
	Violation of local routing policies
Vulnerabilities	Misconfigured routers
	Software vulnerabilities
Attacks	Spoofing
	Message injection
Countermeasures	Multi Protocol Label Switching (MPLS)

Message or data injection refers to injecting arbitrary code to the system. This is used to compromise input validation techniques.

Multi Protocol Label Switching (MPLS) is often referred to as a Layer 2.5 protocol, as it lies between Layers 2 and 3 of the OSI model. It provides greater reliability and support for circuit and packet switching based clients.

Ethernet

It is a family of frame-based networking technologies that is used in a Local Area Network (LAN).

Protocol / Service	Ethernet
Layer(s)	The Ethernet operates in the data link layer and the physical layer of the TCP/IP model.
Applications	The Ethernet initially used co-axial cables for networking
	Present day technologies include hubs or switches and twisted pair cabling
	Ethernet technologies have predominantly replaced other LAN standards such as token ring, FDDI, and ARC net.

Protocol / Service	Ethernet
Threats	Spoofing
Vulnerabilities	Reuse of frame buffers
Attacks	Denial-of-service (DOS)
	Eavesdropping
Countermeasures	Segmentation
	Filtering
	Encryption

Summary

Today our focus was on the transport, network, and link layers of the TCP/IP model. We discussed different layers and their associated protocols. We also covered some specific applications related to protocols such as threats, vulnerabilities, attacks, and countermeasures. We started with the transport layer and protocols such as the TCP and UDP operating in the transport layer. It is important to note that the TCP is used where the reliability of datagram's delivery is important, and the UDP where speed of datagram's delivery is important.

We moved on to discuss the Internet Protocol (IP) which is a connectionless protocol that operates on the Internet layer. This protocol tries the best effort method to deliver data packets across the network. In fact, TCP/IP is named after these two important protocols: TCP and IP. We've also covered the all-important IPsec, which provides end-to-end security and works on the network layer. Remember that IPsec is used for assuring security in the areas of authentication and encryption to the IP-based communications.

Our review then focused on other protocols in the TCP/IP. Examples include the Address Resolution Protocol (ARP) that is used to resolve IP addresses, and the Border Gateway Protocol (BGP) that is a routing protocol operating in the link layer.

It is important to note that Ethernet works both in the data link layer and the physical layer. It is a set of technologies for Local Area Networking (LAN).

Tomorrow we'll move on to the next security domain that deals with security architecture and design.

Practice questions

1. The Internet Protocol (IP) operates in the _____.
    a) Physical layer
    b) Network layer
    c) Application layer
    d) Communication layer

2. The Border Gateway Protocol is a(n) _____.
    a) Physical layer protocol
    b) Address Resolution Protocol
    c) Routing Protocol
    d) LAN technology

3. The Multi Protocol Label Switching (MPLS) is often referred as _____.
    a) Application Layer Protocol
    b) Layer 2.5 protocol
    c) Layer 3 protocol
    d) Layer 3.5 protocol

4. The Media Access Control (MAC) is a(n) _____.
    a) Addressing scheme
    b) Internet protocol
    c) Hardware model
    d) Network Interface card address

5. The Encapsulation Security Payload (ESP) is predominantly used in the _____.
    a) Transmission Control Protocol
    b) IPsec
    c) Ethernet
    d) ARCnet

16

Day 15: Security Architecture and Design

A computer system includes operating systems, equipment, networks, and applications. Based on the information security requirements, a computer system also consists of controls that enforce various levels of confidentiality, integrity, and availability needs of the information. A document that specifies the security requirements and needs to be addressed and maintained in a computer system is known as the **security policy**.

Security architecture and design enforces the security requirements of computer systems as defined in the security policy. Some of the important objectives of this domain are to address the security concepts, principles, structures, and standards for computer architecture and computer systems. These objectives form the baseline for designing, implementing, monitoring, and securing computer systems. This domain also addresses various security models pertaining to computer architecture, assurance mechanisms, guidelines, and standards.

Knowledge requirements

During the next two days, we'll focus on areas that a candidate appearing for the CISSP exam should understand that are related to security architecture and design:

- Computer architecture
- Security mechanism and controls related to computer architecture
- Security mechanism and controls as defined in the Trusted Computer Security Evaluation Criteria (TCSEC)
- Concepts put forth in the Trusted Computer System (TCS) and Trusted Computing Base (TCB)
- System threats, vulnerabilities, and countermeasures
- Trust and assurance models and references

The approach

In accordance with the knowledge expected in the CISSP exam, this domain is broadly divided in the following four sections:

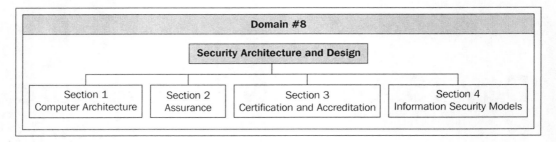

Section 1: This section provides important concepts in the ever-evolving design of computer architecture. As with any other section, our focus is to quickly review important security mechanisms within computer systems.

Section 2: This section deals with assurance-related concepts, specifications, and standards that correspond to specific security needs in computer systems.

Section 3: This section helps us to understand the certification and accreditation schemas, specifications, and processes that are related to computer security.

Section 4: Finally, we'll conclude this important domain with specific focus on the information security models that specify techniques to fulfill requirements of confidentiality, integrity, availability, or a combination of these three tenets for information assets.

Today we will review some of the important security concepts related to computer architecture.

At the end of the day, you should understand and be able to explain the following topics:

- Concepts in computer architecture
- Trusted computing base
- Mechanisms related to the protection domain

Computer architecture

The elements of a computer that are fundamental to its operations, together with the way in which the elements are organised, are referred to as **computer architecture**.

A computer is a physical device consisting of various components. These physical components are known as **hardware**. The hardware components process a set of instructions and data presented to them, which is known as **software**.

Elements of computer architecture

The fundamental elements in computer architecture are the input/output systems, the Central Processing Unit (CPU), and the memory. The common plane that connects these three elements is known as the **bus**.

The functions of each of these elements are as follows:

Input/Output (IO) systems: These systems interface with the CPU. The IO mechanisms and structures enable a supply of input instructions and data to the CPU. It also manages the output data from the CPU to appropriate interfaces.

Central Processing Unit (CPU): It is the heart and brain of a computer. Its primary function is to process the instructions and the data presented to it by other systems, such as application software, through the input or output systems. The process carried out by the CPU is known as executing the program.

Memory: Its function is to store the instructions and data either permanently or temporarily. To this effect, computer memory can be categorized as follows:

- **Primary memory**: Refers to a storage area that is directly addressable by the CPU. Examples of such memory are cache, the Random Access Memory (RAM), and the Read-Only Memory (ROM).
- **Secondary memory**: Refers to a permanent storage that is indirectly accessible by the CPU. Examples of such memory are magnetic disks, tapes, and so on.

Telecommunication and networking technologies enable computers to communicate with each other, or act as a server or a client, or both. Based on the role of a computer in a network, the network architecture is classified as a client-server model or a centralized model. Since interconnectivity is the primary goal, these models are generally known as **distributed architecture**.

Computer systems

The collection of hardware and software together is referred to as a **computer system**.

A computer system can be categorized as an open system, a closed system, or a combination of both.

An open system, as the name implies, is open to interconnectivity with other systems and can be reviewed by independent entities. This means an open system can be reviewed and evaluated by third parties. In contrast, a closed system is proprietary in nature, the internal workings are not known, and auditing such systems (such as code review or architecture review) is not feasible by independent entities.

Computing principles

From the asset classification and information security perspective, a computer is a physical asset and therefore physical security principles are necessary and applicable to it. The service provided by a computer is known as **computing**, and is treated as a service asset.

Various computing methods are available to improve the instruction execution cycle. An instruction execution cycle is the time required to fetch the instructions and data from memory, decode the information, and execute it.

When many operations are performed as per the instruction, then such computing is known as the **Complex Instruction Set Computer (CISC)**. When instruction sets reduce the cycle time to execute instructions, then the method is known as the **Reduced Instruction Set Computer (RISC)**. When the fetch, decode, and execute cycles overlap due to a set of instructions attempting to reduce the time cycle, such a method is known as **pipelining**.

Information security in computer architecture

From the information security perspective, computer architecture should take into consideration the CIA aspects of computing services.

Security policy refers to defining and enforcing the CIA aspects of computing services.

The following are concepts related to the information security aspects of computer architecture.

Trusted computing

As defined by the Orange Book, the **Trusted Computing Base (TCB)** is the totality of protection mechanisms within a computer system, including hardware, firmware, and software. It is this combination which is responsible for enforcing a computer security policy. We covered this concept in *Chapter 11 – Day 10: Operations Security.*

A practical example is the way UNIX-like operating systems, such as the AIX, implement security mechanisms to their TCB. When the TCB option is selected during the installation, the system enables the following:

- **Trusted path**: It is a secure communication path between users and the TCB of the operating system. This path is used by administrators for administering the systems and by users when the data they send needs to be highly protected.

- **Trusted shell**: It is used by users and administrators to run trusted programs.

- **Integrity checking mechanisms for the TCB**: It checks the consistency of the trusted files and its associated files.

The **Trusted Computer System (TCS)** refers to systems that have a well-defined security policy, accountability, assurance mechanisms, and proper documentation.

The Trusted Computer System Evaluation Criteria (TCSEC) is a set of basic requirements that evaluate the effectiveness of computer security controls built into computer systems. The TCSEC is a United States' Department of Defense (DOD) standard, and is popularly known as the Orange Book. We covered the TCSEC in detail in Chapter 11.

Protection domain is a security function to control or prevent direct access by an insecure, or lower-level entity, to a secure, or higher-level entity. Software programs, such as operating systems or applications, either run in a user protection domain or a kernel protection domain.

When the protection domains are organized in a hierarchical format, they are known as **protection rings**. The purpose of protection rings is to protect data, functionality, and the system from malicious behaviors of programs.

Security perimeter is an outer ring of a trusted computing base, or the outer ring, of a protected domain or entity.

Trusted path refers to a secure path provided by software to communicate with entities within the trusted rings in order to eliminate unauthorized access.

Encapsulation is a technique to hide information from unauthorized entities.

Abstraction is the process of hiding the details and exposing only the essential features of a particular concept or object that is encapsulated.

Reference monitor is a secure module that controls access to trusted and protected entities in a TCB.

Security kernel is a computer architecture consisting of hardware and software elements that implement reference monitoring.

Security label is a classification mechanism to indicate the security levels of entities. The labels are low, medium, and high which are based on the sensitivity of data and function.

Logical Security Guard is a security mechanism to control the communication between entities that are labeled low sensitive and high sensitive.

Security modes are operating modes based on the operating level of the information systems along with the sensitivity level or security label. Some of the modes an information system may operate include dedicated, compartmented, controlled, and limited access.

Summary

Today we covered some concepts related to computer architecture. The primary requirement in this domain is the enforcement of security policy pertaining to the architecture and design of computer systems.

A computer system is prone to compromise in terms of confidentiality, integrity, and availability breaches. In order to avoid this, the architecture should enforce certain security mechanisms that prevent unauthorized access by low sensitive entities to high sensitive entities.

The TCSEC, or the Orange Book, advocates a trusted computing base as a requirement. A trusted computing base implements various security mechanisms to protect computer systems. These mechanisms are applicable to security domains, which are segregated as security rings.

Tomorrow we'll move on to discuss the various assurance requirements of trusted systems.

Practice questions

1. A Trusted Computer System should have _____.

    a) A well-defined security policy

    b) Accountability

    c) Assurance mechanisms

    d) All the above three

2. A security label is NOT _____.

    a) A classification mechanism

    b) A labeling of low, medium, high based on sensitivity

    c) A computer model

    d) Used for defining protection mechanisms

3. The process of hiding the details, and exposing only the essential features of a particular concept or object that are encapsulated, is known as _____.

    a) Security domain

    b) Abstraction

    c) Security label

    d) Orange book

4. During the instruction execution cycle, when many operations are performed through a single instruction, then the mechanism is known as _____.

    a) Reduced Instruction Set Computing

    b) Complex Instruction Set Computing

    c) Pipelining

    d) Encapsulation

5. Security ring is a(n) _____.

    a) Outer ring of a security domain

    b) Inner ring of a security domain

    c) Encryption mechanism

    d) Security domain

17

Day 16: Security Architecture and Design

An old adage states "a stitch in time saves nine" or "an ounce of prevention is worth a pound of cure." A good security practice is an analogue to such proverbs. If security is addressed during the design and development stage of an application or product, potential vulnerabilities can be avoided. Security architecture and design is one such domain predominantly concerned with processes and practices that include security requirements at the development stage.

Yesterday we covered some concepts pertaining to computer architecture and trusted computing. Today we'll focus on assurance, standards, system guidelines and system security models that are relevant to security architecture and design. Our focus is on:

- Assurance aspects
- Computer system security assurance standards
- Certification and accreditation standards
- Computer system security models

At the end of the chapter, you should understand and be able to explain the following:

- Concepts in assurance-related standards
- Certification and accreditation schemes
- Computer security models

Assurance

Computer systems are entrusted with data processing and data storage. Security needs increases corresponding to the criticality or sensitiveness of the data being processed or held in computer systems. In information security, the term **assurance** means the level of trust, or the degree of confidence, in the satisfaction of security needs of an application or product. Since organization's develop computer applications or products, the assurance aspects cover the organizations' security practices as well.

As security professionals, we need to observe the following two key words while dealing with assurance processes: "level" as in level of trust, and "degree" as in degree of confidence. If you observe, a level or degree can be a number such as 1, 2, 3, and so on or a letter such as A, B, C, and so on, or any other representation that is hierarchical. Therefore, assurance specifications, standards, or frameworks specify hierarchical levels to distinguish the product or process maturity in meeting the security needs.

In the next section, we'll review some important assurance frameworks that are used in governments and industry.

Common Criteria (CC)

In the previous chapter we covered concepts related to the Trusted Computing Base (TCB). In simple terms, the TCB enforces security based on a protection profile. The Common Criteria (CC) is an assurance framework that defines a protection profile. It is predominantly derived from the following three country-specific standards:

1. The Trusted Computer Security Evaluation Criteria (TCSEC), a US standard.

2. The Information Technology Security Evaluation Criteria (ITSEC), a European standard.

3. The Canadian Trusted Computer Product Evaluation Criteria (CTCPEC), a Canadian standard.

[The international standard **ISO/IEC 15408** is based on Common Criteria.]

The following are concepts related to Common Criteria that you should be aware of:

- **Target of Evaluation** (**TOE**): It's the target product or system that is to be evaluated.

- **Security Target** (**ST**): Principally, it's a document that identifies the security properties of the TOE. This document contains the Security Functions Requirement (SFR), which may be provided by a product or a system.

- **Evaluation Assurance Level** (**EAL**): It's a numerical rating based on the evaluation level and the Security Assurance Requirements (SAR). There are seven levels of the EAL ranging from the EAL1 (the most basic) to the EAL7 (the most stringent) in Common Criteria.

The **Trusted Computer Security Evaluation Criteria** (**TCSEC**) is also known as The *Orange Book* in the Rainbow Series published by the United States Department of Defense (DoD). The focus of the TCSEC is confidentiality. The DoD's other standard is the **Trusted Network Interpretation** (**TNI**), also known as The *Red Book,* which address confidentiality and integrity. We've covered the TCSEC in detail in *Chapter 11 – Day 10: Operations Security.*

The **Information Technology Security Evaluation Criteria** (**ITSEC**) is a European standard for IT security that specifies evaluation criteria for functionality and assurance.

There are two kinds of assurances specified in the ITSEC. They are as follows:

1. Correctness of security functions: Assuring that the security functions support the confidentiality, integrity, and availability requirements.

2. Effectiveness of the Target of Evaluation (TOE): Assuring that the security functions are effective.

The ITSEC divides the evaluation parameters as follows:

- Functionality classes: These are a predefined set of complementary security enforcing functions capable of being implemented in a TOE.

- Assurance levels: These show the level of confidence in the security provided by a TOE.

- Correctness level: This is a property which represents a TOE to accurately reflect the stated security target for a system or product. Overall, there are seven levels in assurance and correctness parameters. The levels range from E0 to E6.

- Security functions: These are functions for assuring the combination of confidentiality, integrity, and availability requirements.

The **Canadian Trusted Computer Product Evaluation Criteria (CTCPEC)** is a Canadian standard for security product evaluation published by the **Communications Security Establishment (CSE)**.

Certification and accreditation

Certification is the process of verification and validation of an approach, based on security requirements by organizations, pertaining to security management. It confirms the adherence to security requirements by documented evidence. **Accreditation** is the act of granting certification.

Let us review some of the certification and accreditation processes related to computer system security.

DITSCAP

The **Department of Defense Information Technology Security Certification and Accreditation Process (DITSCAP)** is a standardized approach designed to guide defense agencies in the USA through the certification and accreditation process for a single IT entity.

There are four phases in the DITSCAP process and are listed as follows:

1. **Definition**: In this phase, all system requirements and capabilities are documented to include the mission, function, and interfaces.

2. **Verification**: The recommended changes to a system are performed in this phase, and the resulting deliverable is a refined System Security Authorization Agreement (SSAA).

3. **Validation**: This phase proceeds with a review of the SSAA.

4. **Post-accreditation**: In this phase, system changes are managed, system operations are reviewed, acceptable risk is maintained, and the SSAA is updated.

 The **System Security Authorization Agreement (SSAA)** is a document that specifies system specifications such as the system mission, target environment, target architecture, security requirements, and applicable data access policies. The SSAA is a base on which certification and accreditation actions take place.

NIACAP

The **National Information Assurance Certification and Accreditation Process** (**NIACAP**) is a process of certification and accreditation for computer systems that handle USA national security information. It is derived from the DITSCAP.

DIACAP

The **DoD Information Assurance Certification and Accreditation Process** (**DIACAP**) is a standard that supersedes the DITSCAP.

SSE-CMM

The **System Security Engineering Capability Maturity Model** (SSE-CMM) is a system security process maturity model. It focuses on requirements pertaining to the implementation of security in a system or a group of systems. It focuses specifically on the IT security domain. It is a sponsored effort of the **National Security Agency** (**NSA**), of the USA.

Security engineering practices

There are 11 security engineering practices that are defined in the SSE-CMM. They are as follows:

Process Area	Base Security Practices	Description
PA01	Administer Security Controls	Ensures that security requirements considered during the system's design stage are actually implemented and are available in the operational systems
PA02	Assess Impact	Identifies and assesses the impact and the likelihood of an occurrence
PA03	Assess Security Risk	Identifies and assesses the likelihood of threats exploiting the vulnerabilities, and the impact of such exposures
PA04	Assess Threat	Identifies and assesses security threats to the system
PA05	Assess Vulnerability	Identifies and assesses a system's security vulnerabilities that could be exploited by threats
PA06	Build Assurance Argument	Identifies and assesses system security vulnerabilities that could be exploited by the threats

Process Area	Base Security Practices	Description
PA07	Coordinate Security	Ensures that all parties are aware of, and are involved with, security engineering activities.
PA08	Monitor Security Posture	Ensures security breaches that are either attempted or are successful, or the mistakes or weaknesses in the system that could breach the security, are identified and reported
PA09	Provide Security Input	Provides relevant security information inputs to security architects, designers, implementers, or users
PA10	Specify Security Needs	Explicitly identify the system's security needs
PA11	Verify and Validate Security	Checks whether solutions meet security requirements, including the customer operational security needs

Security organizational processes

There are also 11 process areas related to project and organizational practices defined in the SSE-CMM. They are listed as follows:

Process Area	Organizational Base Practices	Description
PA12	Ensure Quality	Ensures quality by assurance, as assurance is one of the quality aspects of security. This process takes into account the security engineering practice PA06 (Build assurance argument).
PA13	Manage Configurations	Provides evidence to build an assurance argument. This process takes into account the security engineering practice PA06 (Build assurance argument).
PA14	Manage Project Risks	Identifies, assesses, monitors, and mitigates risks to the success of both the systems engineering activities and the overall technical effort. PA07 (Coordinate security) should be taken into account during this process.
PA15	Monitor and Control Technical Effort	Provides adequate visibility of actual progress and risks pertaining to documented plans. This process takes into account PA01 (Administer security), PA07 (Coordinate security), and PA08 (Monitor security).
PA16	Plan Technical Effort	Establishes plans that provide a basis for scheduling, budgeting, controlling, tracking, and negotiating the nature and scope of the technical work involved in system development, manufacturing, use, and disposal. This process takes into account the security engineering practice PA07 (Coordinate security).

Process Area	Organizational Base Practices	Description
PA17	Define Organization's Systems Engineering Process	Creates and manages the organization's standard system engineering processes. This process takes into account the security engineering practice PA07 (Coordinate security).
PA18	Improve Organization's Systems Engineering Process	Gains a competitive advantage by continuously improving the effectiveness and efficiency of the systems engineering process used by an organization.
PA19	Manage Product Line Evolution	Introduces services, equipment, and new technologies to achieve the maximum benefit of the product evolution.
PA20	Manage Systems Engineering Support Environment	Provides the technology environment needed to develop the product and perform the process. This process takes into account the security engineering practices PA03 (Assess security risk) and PA06 (Build assurance argument).
PA21	Provide Ongoing Skills and Knowledge	Ensures that projects and the organization have the necessary knowledge and skills to achieve the objectives.
PA22	Coordinate with Suppliers	Addresses the needs to effectively manage the portions of product work that are conducted by other organizations. This process takes into account the security engineering practice PA10 (Specify security needs).

Information security models

We're aware that information security is characterized by the preservation of the confidentiality, integrity, and availability of information assets such as computer systems, the data they process, and the associated system and processes. We also know that confidentiality, integrity, and availability are known as the three tenets of information security. Information security models provide a method to protect either the confidentiality, integrity, or availability of information. Certain models provide methods that cover more than one tenet.

In the following section, we will discuss some the popular information security models. These models are predominantly used in government and military systems.

Take-Grant model

This computer security model is also known as the **Take-Grant protection model**. This model specifies how to obtain (Take) rights, or transfer (Grant) the rights, from one entity to another. There are two entities defined in this model—subject and object. In simple terms, this model proposes a **directed graph** that represents the transfer of rights.

There are four rules in this model:

- Take rule—a subject takes rights from another subject
- Grant rule—a subject grants rights to another subject
- Create rule—a subject creates new nodes
- Remove rule—a subject removes its rights over an object

Bell-LaPadula model

It is a **data confidentiality model** developed by David Elliot Bell and Len LaPadula. Since the focus is on confidentiality, this model prescribes access controls to classified or confidential information. It specifies three security properties. The first two are related to the **Mandatory Access Control (MAC)** and the last is the **Discretionary Access Control (DAC)**. We've covered access control techniques in *Chapter 06 – Day 5: Access Control*.

There are three security properties described in this model. Please remember that a security property is sometimes referred to as a security rule. The properties are:

- **Simple Security Property**: It states that a subject at a given security level may not read an object at a higher security level (no read up)
- ***-property (star-property)**: It states that a subject at a given security level must not write to any object at a lower security level (no write down)
- **Discretionary Security Property**: It uses an access matrix to specify the discretionary access control

A simple way to remember this model is: no read up and no write down pertaining to confidentiality.

[This model is also known as the **state machine model** and is predominantly used in governmental and military establishments.]

Biba model

This model, developed by Kenneth J. Biba, focuses on **data integrity**.

It states the following two rules:

- **Simple Integrity Axiom**: A subject at a given level of integrity may not read an object at a lower integrity level (no read down)
- *** (star) Integrity Axiom**: A subject at a given level of integrity must not write to any object at a higher level of integrity (no write up)

A simple way to remember this model is: no read down and no write up pertaining to integrity.

Clark-Wilson Model

This is an integrity model developed by David D. Clarke and David R. Wilson. This model aims to address multi-level security requirements.

Summary

Today we covered some concepts and definitions that are relevant to assurance, certification, accreditation processes, and security models that should be considered while developing a security architecture or designing secure systems.

Tomorrow we'll move on to review important concepts in business continuity planning and disaster recovery processes.

Practice questions

1. The Common Criteria is _____.

   a) A Data Encryption Standard

   b) An information security procedure

   c) Incident management

   d) An assurance framework

2. Which one of the following is NOT an accreditation and certification process?

   a) DITSCAP

   b) NIACAP

   c) Biba Model

   d) DIACAP

3. The Bell-LaPadula model is also known as the _____.

   a) Take-Grant model

   b) Biba model

   c) Confidentiality model

   d) Integrity model

4. The Take-Grant model prescribes _____.

   a) Directed graph of subject and object

   b) No write up

   c) No read up

   d) No read down

5. The Clarke-Wilson model is predominantly concerned with _____.

   a) Confidentiality

   b) Integrity

   c) Availability

   d) Access control

18

Day 17: Business Continuity and Disaster Recovery Planning

Today we will review some of the important concepts in the **Business Continuity** and **Disaster Recovery Planning (DRP)** domain. As the name suggests, this domain is concerned with the continuation of business in the event of a disaster. When we say continuity, it means the continuity of critical business processes. Continuity aspects are not only related to IT systems, but to the overall business and related processes.

Traditionally, **Business Continuity Planning (BCP)** proactively plans the continuation of critical business processes. Business processes may include accounting, payroll, Customer Relationship Management (CRM), and so on. DRP is used to plan for the recovery of information systems that support critical business processes.

Knowledge requirements

The following areas related to business continuity and disaster recovery planning are important in preparation for the CISSP exam:

- Develop and document the scope and the plans
- Understand and conduct the Business Impact Analysis (BIA)
- Understand the strategies related to recovery and development
- Understand the elements that need to be addressed in the plan documents
- Understand the importance of communication and in providing training
- Understand and implement the maintenance of plans

The approach

Based on the knowledge expected in the CISSP exam, this domain is broadly divided into the following two sections:

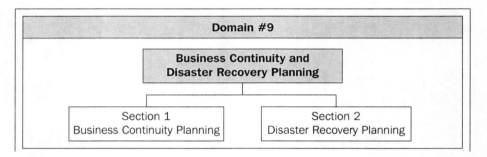

Section 1: This section provides important concepts related to the Business Continuity Planning (BCP) process.

Section 2: This section provides important concepts related to the Disaster Recovery Planning (DRP) process.

Today our focus is on BCP, and at the end of the day you should understand and be able to explain the following:

- Concepts in the BCP domain
- Business continuity goals and objectives
- The Business Impact Analysis (BIA)

Business Continuity Planning (BCP)

Before plunging deeper into the myriad concepts of the BCP and DRP domains, let us review some important concepts in the risk assessment and risk management areas:

1. **Risk** is the probability of a threat exploiting a vulnerability, and the resulting impact. The impact may be related to the loss of money, resources, customer confidence, reputation or legal and regulatory non-compliance, and related issues.

2. A **threat** is an event that could affect business operations or processes.

3. A **vulnerability** is a weakness in the system that could be exploited by a threat.

In the BCP domain, our focus will be on specific threat events that could have devastating impacts on an organization's functionality as a whole and the IT infrastructure in particular. Examples of such events are fires, floods, earthquakes, tornados, terrorist attacks, and so on. Generally, organizations may not have controls to prevent such events. Such events are known as disruptive events. In other words, an event that could impact regular operations for a prolonged period of time can be described as a disruptive event.

Business Continuity Planning (BCP) is a process that proactively addresses the continuation of business operations during, and after, of such disruptive events occur. The aim is in prevent interruptions to operations.

The BCP goals and objectives

BCP requires the coordinated effort by a team of personnel drawn from different business functions within an organization. Let us quickly review the goal and objectives pertaining to the BCP process.

The goal of BCP is to ensure the continuity of business operations without impacting the organization.

While designing the BCP, **availability** should be considered as the most important factor.

People are the most important asset in business operations. Therefore, preventing the loss of human life is one of the primary objectives of the BCP. The other important objective is to avoid any serious damage to business assets or operations.

The BCP process

Business Continuity Planning involves the following processes:

1. **Scoping** in terms of assets, operations, and business processes

   Scoping is an extremely important activity in the BCP process. The scope of BCP is primarily focused on business processes. For example, if the scope of BCP is the Customer Relationship Management (CRM) processes, then we're looking at CRM-related information systems, data, people associated with customer management, the facilities such as the servers, data center, backup media, and so on. By focusing on a business process and defining its scope, we should be able to see an end-to-end link of all the associated assets, operations, and processes. Therefore, the primary criterion of BCP scoping is to ensure that it is **appropriate**, which means ensuring that the scoping process covers all essential and critical resources.

2. **Initiating** the planning process

   The BCP process is initiated by establishing the **roles and responsibilities** of the personnel involved. Generally, a BCP committee is formed with personnel drawn from critical business units. The function of the BCP committee is to create, implement, and test the plans. A critical component in the planning process is the support and involvement of the senior management throughout the process lifecycle.

3. **Performing** the Business Impact Analysis (BIA)

   Business Impact Analysis (BIA) is a type of risk assessment exercise that tries to assess qualitative and quantitative impacts on the business due to a disruptive event. The qualitative impacts are generally operational impacts, such as the inability to deliver products or services, while the quantitative impacts are related to financial losses.

   In general, the BIA uses **What-if** scenarios to assess the risks. For example,

   - **What** will the financial losses be **if** the CRM server is down for four hours?
   - **What** will the operational issues be **if** the system administrator is not available during an emergency update of the system?
   - **What** will the legal issues be **if** the customer data is corrupted or if the customer data is stolen?

   A matrix of What-If scenarios is created and analyzed to develop suitable mitigation strategies for the risks. In the BCP terminology, this risk mitigation strategy is known as a **continuity plan**.

4. Developing the Business Continuity Plans

   The Business Continuity Plans are proactive measures which identify critical business processes that are required for continuity and sustainability of the business. These plans are based on the BIA. For example, let us assume that an organization has a **Service Level Agreement (SLA)** with its customers for a maximum of two hours of continuous downtime of its CRM services. Now, the continuity plans need to proactively address the systems that are needed to ensure adherence to the SLA. The organization needs a strategy, or a plan, that should be consistent across business units. Defining and documenting the **continuity strategy** are two important functions that constitute the development of the Business Continuity Plans.

5. Implementing the Business Continuity Plans, testing them, and creating awareness in the personnel

   The senior management must approve the properly documented Business Continuity Plans. On approval, the implementation of the plans should begin. Personnel associated with business continuity strategy and operations must be made aware of the continuity processes. The plans must periodically be tested and updated based on the lessons learned from such tests.

6. Business Continuity Plan maintenance

   The BCP lifecycle includes maintenance of the plans. The primary driver for plan updates is based on incidents, periodic risk assessments, and changes to the business environment. The plans need to periodically be reviewed and updated based on business changes, technology changes, or policy changes.

BCP best practices

The following best practices are gleaned from many BCP-related standards and guidelines. They form the base of a successful BCP process.

BCP should possess the following qualities:

- **Appropriate**: The scoping process should cover the essential resources
- **Adequate**: Based on the BIA, the adequacy of available resources pertaining to continuity and recovery should be established
- **Complete**: The plan should include all the required resources identified in the analysis

BCP resources should include:

- Availability of processes
- Availability of people to implement the processes

BCP process should include:

- Testing the plans
- The day-to-day functions and activities to be performed in order to make the plan effective and ready all the times

BCP measures should include:

- Preventative measures to control known issues
- Facilitating measures to act in a timely manner on issues that are not under the reasonable control of the organization

BCP should identify:

- Mission-critical systems
- The business impact due to the unavailability of critical systems (loss of revenue, loss of profits, inability to comply with laws, damage to reputation, and so on)
- Preventive controls
- Recovery controls

BCP objectives should include:

- **Recovery Time Objective (RTO)**: A timeframe within which the systems should be recovered (indicated in terms of hours or days)
- **Recovery Point Objective (RPO)**: The maximum period of time, or amount of, transaction data the business can afford to lose during a successful recovery

BCP procedures should include:

- Procedure for testing the plans
- Procedure for updating the plans

BC Plans should contain:

- Notification—To whom, and in case the concerned personnel is not available, who holds the secondary responsibility.

- Call trees—The list of personnel associated with continuity operations and their contact details.

- Response teams—They should respond during a disruptive event. For example, an event such as fire requires trained teams to handle evacuation and other specific procedures.

- Updating mechanism for contacts.

- A step-by-step procedure for recovery.

- Appropriate testing.

- Restoring the primary site to normalcy.

- The required records and their format.

- The awareness of people.

Summary

Today we covered some of the concepts and requirements in the business continuity domain. The primary requirement in this domain is to address the availability of resources during and after disruptive events.

Business Continuity Planning (BCP) is a process to proactively plan the continuation of business operations during and after a disaster. Critical operations and the associated resources, along with their recovery time requirements are identified using the Business Impact Analysis (BIA).

Tomorrow we'll move on to the Disaster Recovery Planning (DRP) process that addresses the actions needing to be performed during and after a disastrous event.

Practice questions

1. The primary focus of the Business Continuity Plan is _____.
    a) Integrity
    b) Authenticity
    c) Availability
    d) Authorization

2. The Business Continuity Planning (BCP) is _____.
    a) Reactive in nature
    b) Preventive in nature
    c) A risk management exercise
    d) Risk tolerance

3. The Business Impact Analysis (BIA) is used to _____.
    a) Ascertain the value of the assets
    b) Ascertain the value of the business
    c) Ascertain the value of the resources
    d) Ascertain the loss to a business due to a threat event

4. The Recovery Time Objective (RTO) estimates _____.
    a) The timeframe within which operations should resume
    b) The costs associated with recovering the operations
    c) The resources required for business continuity
    d) The time required to develop a BC plan

5. The Recovery Point Objective estimates _____.
    a) The timeframe within which to resume operations
    b) The data recovery point
    c) The resources required for business continuity
    d) The time required to develop a Business Continuity Plan

Day 18: Business Continuity and Disaster Recovery Planning

19

Today we'll cover some important concepts in the Business Continuity and Disaster Recovery Planning domain. Traditionally, Business Continuity Planning (BCP) proactively plans, implements, and tests for the continuity of critical business processes. As stated in the previous chapter, business processes may include accounting, payroll, Customer Relationship Management (CRM), and so on. The Disaster Recovery Planning (DRP) is useful for planning the recovery of information systems that support the critical business processes.

In this chapter we'll focus on the following topics:

- Disaster Recovery Planning processes
- Disaster recovery teams
- Backup concepts
- Alternate sites
- Testing and maintaining a disaster recovery plan

By the end of this day, you should comprehend and be able to explain the following:

- Disaster recovery planning process
- Backup concepts
- Alternatives in resuming business from alternate sites

Disaster Recovery Planning (DRP)

Disaster recovery is a process that enables a business to recover operations from an event that affects the normal business operations for a prolonged period of time.

At this point, I would like to highlight the similarities and differences between the BCP and the DRP processes:

- Both BCP and DRP are targeted at the continuity or resumption of business processes and operations.
- Both planning processes address actions to be taken when an incident happens or a disruptive event strikes.
- BCP focuses on the continuity of business processes. For example, power failure is an incident, not a disastrous event. BCP will address continuity processes such as the **Uninterrupted Power Supply (UPS)** system, or a power generator. However, BCP focuses on the continuity of the business processes from a holistic perspective of the business.
- DRP focuses on recovery procedures in the aftermath of disastrous events. For example, an earthquake striking the location. This is different from the scenario of a power failure. Therefore, having a UPS system, or generator, will not help. DRP will resume the critical business processes from an alternative site.

Disaster Recovery Planning (DRP) is a process to:

1. Develop procedures that define the actions to be taken during and after a disastrous event.
2. Test the procedures for effectiveness.
3. Update the procedures to reflect the lessons learned from the testing process.

Goals and objectives

The **goal** of DRP is to effectively manage operations during and after a disaster and ensure proper coordination of different teams.

The **objective** of DRP is to continue the business, or IT operations, in a secondary site during a disaster and to restore the primary site in a timely manner.

Components of disaster recovery planning

Some components of disaster recovery include:

- Identification of suitable teams that coordinate the recovery process
- Resumption of business from alternate sites, or recovering data from backup
- Communication with employees, external groups, and media
- Financial management, including insurance

Recovery teams

In disaster recovery, various teams play important roles. The most important teams are:

1. **Recovery team**: On declaration of a disaster, this team is entrusted with the responsibility of implementing the recovery procedures.
2. **Salvage team**: This team is responsible for returning business operations to the primary site.

Recovery sites

A **primary site** is the location(s) where normal business operations, including IT operations, take place.

A **secondary site** is referred to as a backup to the primary site. Generally, secondary sites are located in a different geographic location.

Business resumption from alternative sites

The following are some disaster recovery activities related to the continuation of business operations from an alternative site:

- A **reciprocal agreement** is an arrangement with another company having additional computing facilities that can be utilized during a disaster. The term "reciprocal" implies that it is a mutual agreement where both the companies may utilize the computing facilities of the other in the event of a disaster.
- Another type of arrangement is **subscription services**. It requieres paying, or subscribing to, facility management services that use third-party backup and processing facilities.

The following are certain types of subscription services a company may utlize based on the Business Impact Analysis (BIA), Recovery Time Objectives (RTO), and Recovery Point Objectives (RPO).

 BIA, RTO, and RPO are explained in *Chapter 18 – Day 17: Business Continuity and Disaster Recovery Planning*.

- **Hot sites** are alternate backup sites that are fully configured with computer systems, **Heating**, **Ventilation** and **Air Conditioning** (**HVAC**), and power supply. This type of site also contains all the applications and data to commence operations immediately. Hot sites are highly expensive. Typically, a business operation that needs to be resumed within 24 hours would consider a hot site.

- **Cold sites** contain no computers or other computing equipments. Only HVAC and power are available. The computers and computing equipment, as well as applications and data, need to be installed before commencing operations. Cold sites are the least expensive option. Typically, a business operation that can be resumed in a span of 7 to 10 days would consider this option.

- **Warm sites** are in-between hot and cold sites. In this type of arrangement, computing facilities such as computers, other communication elements, HVAC, and power are available. However, applications and data need to be installed before commencing operations. This type of site is less expensive than hot sites. Typically, a business operation that needs to be restored within a span of 24 to 96 hours would consider this option.

- **Dual sites** refer to mirroring the exact operations and data in alternative sites. From the recovery perspective, this type of site allows instantaneous business resumption. However, such sites are the most expensive option to maintain. Typically, business operations that cannot afford any downtime at all would consider this option.

Backup terminologies

The following concepts are applicable to hot and dual sites in terms of backup and restoration:

- **Electronic vaulting** is a batch process to dump data to a remote backup system at periodical intervals.

- **Remote journaling** is a parallel processing system that writes data in a remote system at the alternate site. This type of backup is used where the RTO is minimal and a high degree of fault tolerance is required.

- **Database shadowing** is used to duplicate data into multiple sites from the remote journaling process. This type of system is used where the fault tolerance requirement is of the highest degree.

Testing procedures

Disaster recovery plans should include various testing procedures to ensure the plans can be tested for adequacy and correctness. The lessons learned from such tests should be incorporated in the plans for better preparedness during a disaster.

The following are some of the industry standard tests pertaining to the DRP process:

- **Checklist review** is a review process for checking the disaster recovery plan by managers of various business units. The following table shows a general checklist. This is a macro level list. Further lists should be generated at lower, micro levels to drill down to finer details.

	Disaster Recovery Planning - General Checklist	
1	Is an updated diagram of network connections and devices available?	☐
2	Is an updated diagram of network connections and devices for DR site available?	☐
3	Is the DR network tested and are the results documented?	☐
4	Are patches applied to DR site systems?	☐
5	Does the DR Plan document specify the information systems to be available in the DR site? (for example: Accounting system, CRM, etc.,)	☐
6	Does the DR Plan specify the applications and the data to be available in the DR site?	☐
7	Is backup data available at the DR site?	☐
8	Is backup based on recovery requirements as per the DR Plan?	☐
9	Is backup data tested frequently for integrity? (sanity checks to see the data is not corrupted)	☐
10	Is a service contacts list is available?	☐
11	Does the DR Plan identify resource allocation such as equipments and communication?	☐
12	Does the DR Plan identify the staff allocation at remote sites?	☐

- **Structured walk-through** is a **tabletop exercise**: In this exercise, the management team of various business units meet and review each step in a sequential manner. Any deficiencies, or missing steps, are discussed and updated in the plan. A checklist review is used to check the availability of resources such as documents, systems, people, communication facilities, backup, and so on. A structured walk-through checks the recovery processes step-by-step, albeit over a tabletop review.

- **Simulation test**: A testing process to simulate an event in a testing environment. This test is expected to provide vital inputs from the actions of various response teams. Any deficiencies can be corrected, including the training requirements. This type of test is also known as **walk-through test** or **drill**. Simulation testing is more comprehensive than the tabletop exercise.

- **Parallel test**: A testing process to test the coordination of other essential groups such as medical, fire services including internal teams, and the adherence to communication procedures. This practice tests the functionality of the plans. Therefore, it is referred to as **functional drill**.

- **Full test**: This type of test tries to simulate a real emergency or disastrous event. It involves participation of all associated teams and groups, as well as real shutdown of primary site, and commencement of operations from the remote site.

Summary

Today we covered some concepts in the Business Continuity and Disaster Recovery Planning domain. DRP consists of a recovery strategy and its corresponding documentation. We've seen that the recovery strategy is based on the Business Impact Analysis (BIA). We've also discussed how a recovery strategy is developed with the objectives of recovery time and recovery point. These two objectives are known as the **Recovery Time Objective (RTO)** and the **Recovery Point Objective (RPO)**.

Therefore, based on the recovery strategy, we can deduce that the primary requirement in this domain is to recover the business operations during and after a disaster event within the recovery timeframe. It is also important to understand that the disaster recovery process is related to restoring the business operations to the primary site from a secondary site within the acceptable timeframe.

Tomorrow we'll cover important concepts in the legal, regulations, compliance, and investigations domain.

Practice questions

1. The role of recovery team is to _____.

   a) Salvage the systems from the primary site

   b) Implement recovery procedures

   c) Communicate with the management

   d) Back up the data

2. The role of salvage team is to _____.

   a) Restore operations to the primary site

   b) Restore operations to secondary site

   c) Communicate with the management

   d) Communicate with the external groups

3. Remote journaling is NOT _____.

   a) A backup methodology

   b) A checklist

   c) A parallel process to write data in the alternate site

   d) For high fault tolerance

4. The simulation test is also known as _____.

   a) A walk-through test

   b) Electronic vaulting

   c) Fault tolerance

   d) Tabletop exercise

5. Which one of the following is the most expensive to maintain?

   a) Hot site

   b) Dual site

   c) Warm site

   d) Cold site

20

Day 19: Legal, Regulations, Compliance, and Investigations

Today our focus will be on computer laws, regulations, compliance, and investigations. Computer-related crimes are on the rise and are presently causing organizations to lose millions of dollars. Organized crime and cyber terrorism are lurking everywhere due to a lack of boundaries on the Internet. Therefore, security professionals need to be aware of various legal and regulatory requirements pertaining to the ethical usage of computers, compliance frameworks across the world, and investigative mechanisms to identify, protect, and preserve any evidence from computer crimes.

Knowledge requirements

A candidate appearing for the CISSP exam should have knowledge in the following areas that relate to the legal, regulations, compliance, and investigation domain:

- International computer crime laws and regulations
- Ethical issues and the code of conduct for security professionals
- Incident handling procedures
- Code of ethics RFC 1087 and (ISC)^2 code of ethics
- Investigations
- Forensic procedures

The approach

In accordance with the knowledge expected in the CISSP exam, this domain is broadly divided into the following five sections:

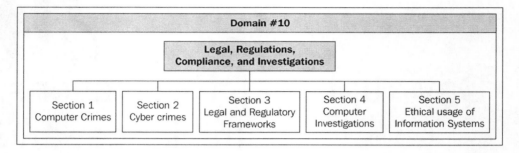

Section 1: This section provides a definition for computer crimes and explains the various types of computer crimes.

Section 2: This section provides a definition for cyber crimes and explains the various types of cyber crimes.

Section 3: This section provides an overview of the various regulatory frameworks and standards across the world which are related to computer and cyber crimes.

Section 4: This section deals with the investigation aspects of computer and cyber crimes.

Section 5: This section covers some important concepts and information related to the ethical usage of computer systems.

Today we'll review some important security concepts related to computer and cyber crimes.

At the end of the day, you should understand and be able to explain the following topics:

- Various computer crimes
- Various cyber crimes
- Various types of attacks

Computer crimes

A computer crime is a fraudulent activity that is perpetrated against computers or IT systems. Motivations for computer crimes could be financial gain, competitive gain, popularity, fame, or adventure.

In computer crime, the term "computer" refers to the role it plays in different scenarios. It could be a crime committed against a computer, or a crime using a computer, or a computer could be incidental in the crime, or a combination of the above three.

Let's look at some common computer crimes. Remember that the end result of a crime is a compromise or breach of Confidentiality, Integrity, and Availability (CIA).

Fraud

Fraud in computer security refers to the manipulation of computer records for creating an advantage or financial gain. Some manipulation techniques include data diddling, salami slicing, and deliberate circumvention of computer security systems such as cracking or unethical hacking.

Data diddling is a malicious activity of changing data during the input or processing stage of a software program to obtain a financial gain.

Salami slicing, also known as **penny shaving**, is the fraudulent activity of regularly siphoning an extremely small quantity of money so as to prevent from being observed or caught.

Hacking refers to discovering the vulnerabilities, holes, or weaknesses in computer software and associated IT systems in order to exploit them to compromise the security or to commit international frauds. A person performing such an activity is known as a **hacker**.

Black hat hackers are people with malicious intents who compromise computer systems to commit crime. Such hackers are known as **crackers** and the malicious hacking activity they perform is known as **cracking**.

White hat hackers, also known as **Ethical hackers**, try to compromise computer systems in order to discover any vulnerabilities or holes and improve the security.

Grey hat hackers are hackers whose intentions and purposes of hacking is ambiguous or unknown.

Theft

Identity theft means stealing someone's identity. The intention is to commit fraud, or misuse a system, while pretending to be someone else. Stealing passwords, login credentials, and credit card information are examples of identity theft.

Cyber stalking means committing fraud by pretending to be a legitimate entity. It is a type of identity theft.

Intellectual property theft is stealing software code or designs for financial gain or creating a competitive advantage.

Malware or Malicious code

Malware is "malicious software" that is designed to compromise, damage, or affect the general functioning of computers, gain unauthorized access, collect private and sensitive information, and corrupt the data.

Viruses, worms, Trojan horses, and spyware such as keyloggers are examples of malware. Writing or spreading malware is also a computer crime.

A **computer virus** is a malicious program or code that attaches itself to files. It can spread from one file to another file as well as from one computer to another. Technically, a virus can spread, or infect the computer, if the user opens an infected file.

Worms are similar to viruses. But unlike viruses, they are self-replicating and propagating computer programs. This means worms do not require human intervention such as opening an infected file.

A **Trojan horse** is a malware that hides its identity within a legitimate program. Users will be tricked into opening the file containing the malware using social engineering.

 Social engineering is a term used for obtaining information through social means. An example is tricking an operator to reveal some organizational information that cannot be obtained by normal means. Social engineering is predominantly non-technical. In the context of a Trojan horse, the tricking is performed by social engineering.

Spyware is malicious code that tracks a user's actions. Examples of user's actions include web browsing patterns, files opened, applications accessed, and so on. Spyware can best be explained as snooping software.

Keyloggers, as the name implies, are a type of spyware that captures keystrokes and transmits them to an attacker's server. Sensitive information, such as usernames and passwords, are captured using keyloggers.

Cyber crime

Criminal activities that are perpetrated using communication networks such as the Internet, telephone, wireless, satellite, and mobile networks are known as **cyber crimes**.

The following are types of cyber crime:

- **Cyberterrorism**: Refers to premeditated attacks on computers and computer networks with an intention to cause harm or further social, ideological, religious, political, or similar objectives.

- **Information warfare:** Use and manage information in pursuit of a competitive advantage over an opponent. The intention is to destabilize the opponent.

- **Denial-of-Service (DoS) attack** or **Distributed Denial-of-Service (DDoS) attack**: In this type of attack, a company's website is flooded with service requests and the site overloads, slows down, or crashes completely.

- **Child pornography**: This type of cyber crime includes making, and digitally distributing, child pornography.

- **Copyright Violation**: This type of cyber crime includes digitally distributing and storing copyrighted materials of others without the copyright owner's explicit permission.

- **Unsolicited Commercial Emails (UCE)**: This type of cyber crime uses email communication to disrupt or send unsolicited commercial emails, or induce the user to perform certain actions to steal information or money.

The following are examples of email-related cyber crimes:

- **Spamming**: Sending unsolicited commercial email is known as spamming. It is a cyber crime that clogs networks and intrudes into the privacy of the users.

- **Phishing**: It is a cyber crime in which a user is lured to open a file attachment containing malware. Additionally, he may be lured to visit an attacker-constructed malicious web site that may look like a legitimate website. The intention is to capture user credentials.

- **Pharming**: It is an attack that redirects a user accessing a legitimate website to an attacker-constructed malicious site without the acceptance or knowledge of the user.

- **SMiShing**: It is a social engineering technique similar to phishing. Instead of email, **Short Messaging Service (SMS)** in mobile telephones is used to perpetrate this cyber crime.

Computer crime related incidents

There are many instances of large scale attacks on computer systems. Most of these attacks are related to DoS and some are also related to confidentiality and integrity breachs. We'll review some of them and their root causes.

Slammer worm

This worm exploits a simple vulnerability known as a "buffer overflow" of a particular database management system. This worm once brought almost half of the global Internet down in a matter of approximately six hours.

Code Red worm

It is a worm originally unleashed in 2001 that attacked web server software of a particular manufacturer. This worm exploited the buffer overflow vulnerability. It propagated very quickly and doubled every 37 minutes.

Mellisa virus

This virus, released in the year 1999, spreads through email attachments.

419 scam

419 scam, also known as the **Nigerian scam**, originates as a spam message luring the user to contact the fraudster for a share of some obscure money. The crime here is phishing.

DDoS attacks

Many Internet websites have regularly been subjected to Distributed Denial-of-Service (DDoS) attacks.

Summary

Today we covered some concepts in the domain of computer and cyber crime.

We primarily discussed how a computer crime can be classified into divisions based on three different scenarios and their combination: a computer crime is committed **against a computer**, or **using a computer**, or a **computer is incidental** in a crime. The primary motives of such crimes is financial gain or to gain a competitive advantage.

Tomorrow we'll move on to discuss legal and regulatory frameworks against computer crimes around the world. We'll also look into investigation mechanisms for identifying, collecting, preserving evidences, and the ethical usage of computing resources.

Practice questions

1. Malware is _____.

   a) Utility software

   b) An operating system

   c) A malicious software

   d) An attack

2. Cyber Crime is using _____.

   a) Communication networks to perpetrate crimes

   b) Phishing techniques

   c) Spam emails

   d) Unauthorized access

3. The primary objective of a Denial-of-Service attack is to compromise _____.

   a) Authenticity

   b) Availability

   c) Authorization

   d) Access Control

4. Keyloggers capture _____.

   a) Key strokes

   b) Documents

   c) Email attachments

   d) Log files

5. Salami slicing is also known as _____.

   a) Penny slicing

   b) Penny storing

   c) Penny sorting

   d) Penny shaving

21

Day 20: Legal, Regulations, Compliance, and Investigations

Yesterday we reviewed different computer crimes including cyber crimes. We also reviewed examples of the incidents that have had a devastating effect on computer installations.

Today we'll focus on the following areas pertaining to the legal, regulations, compliance, and investigations domain.

In this chapter we'll discuss the following topics:

- Different legal systems across the world and specific laws related to information systems
- Concepts in the computer investigations domain
- Using of information systems ethically

At the end of the day, you should comprehend and be able to explain the following:

- Information systems related laws and regulations across the world.
- Concepts related to computer investigations.
- Ethical usage of information systems as prescribed by international bodies, including (ISC)². (ISC)² is an international consortium that administers and manages the CISSP exam and certification.

Legal and regulatory frameworks

Legal and regulatory frameworks are abounding with many terms and jargons that a security professional should be aware of. The following are some that are relevant to the "Information Security" domain.

Law terminologies

Law terminologies are based on the legal systems used. The following are the most important legal systems used by countries across the world:

1. **Common law**: This law was developed on the basis of the decisions of courts and tribunals rather than through statutory laws (legislative statutes). The legal system that uses Common law is known as **common law legal systems**. Countries such as the United Kingdom, most states of United States of America (USA), Canada, Australia, South Africa, India, Malaysia, Singapore, Hong Kong, and so on. These are some of the Common law categories:

    ° **Regulatory law**: It primarily deals with regulations of the administrative agencies of government. It is also known as **administrative law**.

    ° **Criminal law**: It deals with the violations of the government laws. These laws are filed by government agencies against an individual or an organization. The punishment under Criminal law includes imprisonment as well as financial penalties.

    ° **Civil law**: It deals with lawsuits filed by private parties such as corporations or individuals. Punishments under this law are financial and punitive damages.

2. **Statutory law**, **legislative statute**, or **statute law**: It is a law that is set down by legislature or an executive branch of government. Sometimes, a statutory law is also termed **codified law**.

3. **Religious law**: It is a law based on religious principles. Examples include Hindu, Islam, and Christian laws.

4. **Civil law**: It is a legal system based on codes and legislative statutes as opposed to common law. France, Germany, and many other countries in the world practice civil laws.

 Under the Common law there is a Civil law category, which should not be confused with the above.

Intellectual property laws

Intellectual Property (IP) refers to creative works produced by using the intellect or mind. Works such as music, literary works, arts, inventions, symbols, and designs are a part of intellectual property. The creator of such intellectual works has certain exclusive rights over his or her property. These exclusive rights are known as **Intellectual Property Rights (IPR)**.

The **Intellectual property law** is a legal domain that deals with IPR.

Some of the Intellectual Property Rights are as follows:

- **Copyright** is an intellectual property that grants exclusive rights to the creator of an original work. Such rights include deriving financial benefits from works, ownership credits, and so on. Others do not have the "right to copy" such works. Copyright is country-specific. For example, a book written by an author usually falls under the copyright of the author or publisher.

- A **Patent** is a set of exclusive rights granted to the inventor of new, useful, inventive, and industry-applicable inventions. This right excludes others from making, using, selling, or importing the invention. A patent is granted for a specific period of time, and is a public document. For example, a unique method to prevent data theft can be patented.

- A **Trademark** is a unique symbol, or mark, used by individuals or organizations to uniquely represent product or a service. A trademark is also used to distinguish products and services from those of other entities. For example, CISSP is a trademark owned by (ISC)².

- A **Trade secret** is a formula, design, process, practice, or pattern that is not revealed to others. This is done so that information can note be copied and taken to gain a competitive advantage of. For example, the formula of Coca-Cola, the popular soft drink, is a trade secret.

Privacy

Privacy is the need to protect information about individuals, or a group of individuals, from disclosure, or the selective disclosure of information based on individual preferences.

Privacy laws deal with protecting and preserving the rights of an individual's, or a group of individuals', privacy.

Act

An **act** is a law enacted by the legislation or parliament. There are many acts enacted by various governments pertaining to information systems control, compliance, and security.

The following are some of the important ones:

Sarbanes-Oxley Act (SOX), USA

- This act was signed into law in 2002 and is named after its authors, Senator Paul Sarbanes and Representative Paul Oxley.

- This act mandates a number of reforms to enhance corporate responsibility, financial disclosures, and combat corporate and accounting fraud.

- From an information security perspective, the primary requirement is to establish internal controls over financial reporting. This act mandates companies to establish an infrastructure that is designed to protect and preserve records and data from destruction, loss, unauthorized alteration, or other misuse.

Health Insurance Portability and Accountability Act (HIPAA), USA

- This act is a privacy law that is concerned with the privacy of healthcare information.

- Title I of the HIPAA protects health insurance coverage for workers and their families when they change or lose their jobs.

- Title II requires the **Department of Health and Human Services (HHS)** to establish national standards for electronic healthcare transactions and national identifiers for providers, health plans, and employers.

- There are two main rules in the HIPAA — one related to privacy and the other to security:

  - The **privacy rule** mandates the protection and enhancement of the rights of consumers by providing them access to their health information and controlling inappropriate use of that information.

  - The **security rule** mandates organizations to ensure that their electronic healthcare information is secure and confidential.

Gramm Leach Bliley Act (GLBA), USA

- This act was signed into law in 1999. It is concerned with financial services regulation.

- This act requires financial institutions to make certain disclosures about their privacy policies and also gives individuals an opt-out capability.

- This act also criminalizes the practice known as **pretexting**. Pretexting occurs when someone misrepresents themselves to collect information regarding a third party from a financial institution.

Data Protection Act (DPA), UK

- This act creates it a legal requirement for businesses to collect, hold, and process personal data in a secure way.

- It outlines important principles for safeguarding information about people.

Information Technology Act (ITA-2000), India

- The Information Technology Act was enacted by the Indian Parliament in June, 2000.

- The purpose of the act is to promote the use of digital signatures for the growth of e-commerce and e-governance.

- It provides legal recognition to electronic records and also lays down penalties for cyber crimes.

Computer investigations

Computer investigations, also known as **computer forensics**, deal with collecting, preserving, and producing evidences related to computer crimes that are admissible in a court of law.

Evidence in computer investigations is a piece of information that supports a conclusion. From the legal perspective, evidence may be oral or written statements, physical objects, computer files, computer data, or other documentary material admissible in the court of law.

Most evidence that pertains to computer crimes is intangible in nature. It may be stored on a magnetic medium such as a tape or disk drive, or in memory. Information such as the location, time, discovering, securing, controlling and maintaining the evidence need to be followed. This activity is known as a **chain of evidence**.

The cycle of activities from the discovery of evidence to its preservation, transportation, admission in the court, and its return to the owner is known as the **evidence life cycle**.

Ethical usage of information systems

The Ethical usage of information systems relates to the correct usage that complies with the standards, acts, laws, and guidelines. Some organizations that promote information security through research, education, and certification issue a code of ethics for its members. Let us focus on the "code of ethics" issued by the (ISC)² to which its members must adhere.

(ISC)² Code of ethics

(ISC)² is a global leader in information security related certifications. CISSP is one certification offered by the (ISC)². A candidate should become a member of the (ISC)² to appear for the CISSP exam, and once obtained, the candidate should maintain the CISSP certification.

At this juncture, it is important that a candidate should adhere to the "code of ethics" published by the (ISC)².

The goals of the code of ethics, as extracted from the *(ISC)² website*, are as follows:

- Protect society, the commonwealth, and the infrastructure
- Act honorably, honestly, justly, responsibly, and legally
- Provide diligent and competent service to principals
- Advance and protect the profession

The following is an expansion pertaining to these goals:

Protect society, the commonwealth, and the infrastructure

- Promote and preserve public trust and confidence in information and systems
- Promote the understanding and acceptance of prudent information security measures
- Preserve and strengthen the integrity of public infrastructure
- Discourage unsafe practices

Act honorably, honestly, justly, responsibly, and legally

- Tell the truth. Make all stakeholders aware of your actions on a timely basis.

- Observe all contracts and agreements, expressed or implied.

- Treat all members fairly. In resolving conflicts, consider public safety and duties to principals, individuals, and the profession in that order.

- Give prudent advice. Avoid raising unnecessary alarm or giving unwarranted comfort. Take care to be truthful, objective, cautious, and within your competence.

- When resolving differing laws in different jurisdictions, give preference to laws of the jurisdiction in which you render your service.

Provide diligent and competent service to principals

- Preserve the value of their systems, applications, and information

- Respect their trust and the privileges that they grant you

- Avoid conflicts of interest or the appearance thereof

- Render only those services for which you are fully competent and qualified

Advance and protect the profession

- Sponsor for professional advancement those best qualified. All other things equal, prefer those who are certified and who adhere to these canons. Avoid professional association with those whose practices or reputation might diminish the profession.

- Take care not to injure the reputation of other professionals through malice or indifference.

- Maintain your competence. Keep your skills and knowledge current. Give your time and knowledge generously in training others.

Summary

In this last chapter we covered some of concepts in the legal, regulations, compliance, and investigations domain. Legal and regulatory frameworks across the world follow one or more of the Common laws or Civil Laws.

We've seen that Criminal law relates to actions initiated by the government agencies against the violation of government laws. Additionally, Civil law relates to legal suits between individuals and organizations.

As an information security professional, we're predominantly concerned with the IP laws, which address the protection of exclusive rights enjoyed by the inventor of the intellectual property.

We've also covered Privacy laws that are concerned with the protection of information related to individuals.

Finally, we've concluded this chapter with a discussion about computer investigations. The most important point is that computer investigations rely on evidence, which is a piece of information that is admissible in the court of law.

With this we conclude our journey of reviewing the ten information security domains important to understand for the CISSP examination. Tomorrow you can try a sample test with 250 questions that simulate test paper.

Practice questions

1. The Common law was _____.

    a) Developed through statutory laws

    b) Developed through regulatory statutes

    c) Developed based on the decisions of courts

    d) Developed through evidence

2. The Intellectual Property is the _____.

    a) Creative works produced using hands

    b) Creative works produced using eyes

    c) Creative works produced using legs

    d) Creative works produced using intellect

3. Someone misrepresenting themselves to collect information regarding a third party from a financial institution is known as _____.

    a) Hypertexting

    b) Multitexting

    c) Pretexting

    d) Indexing

4. In computer investigation, a piece of information that supports a conclusion is known as _____.

    a) Incidence

    b) Evidence

    c) Conductance

    d) Rule

5. Which one of the following is not an ethic prescribed by the (ISC)^2 code of ethics?

    a) Provide diligent and competent service to principals

    b) Advance and protect the profession

    c) Don't make certain disclosures about the privacy policies

    d) Protect society, the commonwealth, and the infrastructure

22

Day 21: Mock Test Paper

This book has systematically explained all ten domains important from the perspective of the CISSP exam. All along, we have revised these domains and here is a mock test paper that will help you to estimate your understanding of the concepts. It will boost your confidence and prepare you for the real exam. All the best!

Questions

1. An attack that compromises the information stored in a client machine by web browsers for faster retrieval during subsequent visits is known as _____.

   A. Path traversal

   B. Data structure attacks

   C. Eavesdropping

   D. Cache poisoning

2. Which one of the following is not a risk management process?

   A. Risk assessment

   B. Risk exposure

   C. Risk treatment

   D. Risk acceptance

3. The primary criterion of a Business Continuity Planning is to ensure that the scoping is _____.

   A. Adequate

   B. Large

   C. Appropriate

   D. Widely covered

4. If you need to address multilevel security requirements, which of the following models will you choose?

   A. The Take-Grant model

   B. The Bell-LaPadula model

   C. The Biba model

   D. The Clark-Wilson model

5. What is the algorithm used by Wi-Fi Protected Access 2 (WPA2) protocol for encryption?

   A. RC4

   B. Data Encryption Algorithm (DES)

   C. Advanced Encryption Algorithm (AES)

   D. Triple-DES

6. Measurements help in reducing the frequency and severity of security-related issues. Which one of the following is not a right choice for measurements?

   A. Expectations from data privacy requirements

   B. Reduction in the number of incidents

   C. More number of non-conformities during internal or external audits

   D. Expectations from confidentiality requirements of information

7. Birthday attack, a cryptographic attack, guesses a random input data. On which one of the following mathematical probability theories is such an attack based?

   A. There is a chance that more than 50% of randomly chosen people in a group of 23 may have the same birthday.

   B. There is a chance that less than 50% of randomly chosen people in a group of 23 may have the same birthday.

   C. There is a chance that 50% of randomly chosen people in a group of 23 may have the same birthday.

   D. There is a chance that more than 80% of randomly chosen people in a group of 23 may have the same birthday.

8. If an attack uses a combination of brute force and dictionary entries to crack a password, then such an attack is known as a _____.

   A. Replay attack

   B. Password attack

   C. Session hijack

   D. Hybrid attack

9. Identify from the following list an activity that best describes a management control.

    A. Review of security controls

    B. System documentation

    C. Network protection

    D. Personnel security

10. Which of the following encryption standard is proposed to be an official successor of the Data Encryption Standard (DES)?

    A. Triple-DES

    B. Advance Encryption Standard (AES)

    C. Blowfish

    D. Twofish

11. Brute forcing of passwords is a _____.

    A. Probabilistic technique

    B. Path traversal attack

    C. Protocol manipulation

    D. Boundary error

12. Which one of the following may not be a step in computer system startup and shutdown procedures?

    A. The shutdown procedures should ensure that the system shuts down completely during system halt.

    B. Based on security requirements the system startup procedures activate network connections in manual or automatic mode.

    C. Deciding the floor to relocate the computer in case of a virus attack

    D. Checking all the cables before the startup to ensure that they are not loose.

13. Which property of a TCP implementation is vulnerable to Denial-of-Service attacks?

    A. Session establishment

    B. Three-way handshake mechanism

    C. ICMP access

    D. Multicasting

14. While identifying the security awareness training needs, which one of the following is not a wrong choice to consider?

    A. Profit and loss of the organization

    B. Security policies of the organization

    C. Partners and subsidiaries

    D. Number of resellers

15. Which one the following types of hackers are most likely to compromise an organization's computer systems to perpetrate a computer crime for financial gain?

    A. Black hat hackers

    B. White hat hackers

    C. Ethical hackers

    D. Vulnerability assessors

16. Which one of the following is false pertaining to lighting?

    A. Lighting is a reactive control.

    B. Lighting is a deterrent control.

    C. For critical areas, the suggested illumination is two-feet wide and eight-feet tall.

    D. Lighting discourages intruders.

17. Which one of the following choices is a popular algorithm used in asymmetric key encryption, and is a product of two large prime numbers that derives the key pairs?

    A. Rivest, Shamir, and Adleman (RSA)

    B. Blowfish

    C. Twofish

    D. Diffie-Hellman

18. An organization monitors the log-on sessions of its employees. As per the legal requirements and the system monitoring policy of the organization, it is mandatory that the employee is informed and reminded time-to-time about session monitoring. Select the most appropriate method for implementing such a requirement.

    A. Policy document on the intranet

    B. Employee handbook

    C. Wall posters

    D. Log-on banners

19. The ping of death is an example of _____.

    A. Denial-of-Service attack

    B. Protocol manipulation attack

    C. Man-in-the-middle attack

    D. Spoofing attack

20. In information security, the level of trust, or the degree of confidence, on computer systems is know as _____.

    A. Auditing

    B. Assessment

    C. Assurance

    D. Accreditation

21. The Common Vulnerabilities and Exposures (CVE) contains the details of published vulnerabilities. These details are known as _____.

    A. Dictionary of vulnerabilities

    B. Database of vulnerabilities

    C. List of vulnerabilities

    D. Vulnerability exposures

22. A time condition in web applications where the state of a resource changes between the time the resource is checked to the time when it is accessed is known as _____.

    A. A resource management error

    B. An SQL injection

    C. A race condition

    D. A covert channel

23. In public key cryptography, a message is encrypted using the recipient's public key and is decrypted using the recipient's private key. This process ensures which tenet of information security?

    A. Confidentiality

    B. Integrity

    C. Availability

    D. Authenticity

24. An attack that redirects a user accessing a legitimate web site to an attacker-constructed malicious site without the acceptance or knowledge of the user is known as _____.

    A. Phishing

    B. SMiShing

    C. Fishing

    D. Pharming

25. Boundary condition errors result in _____.

    A. Buffer overflow

    B. Buffer reset

    C. Segmentation fault

    D. System reset

26. Which one of the following is not a backup process?

    A. Electronic vaulting

    B. Electronic scaling

    C. Remote journaling

    D. Database shadowing

27. The process of packaging the data packets received from applications is known as encapsulation. What is the term that denotes the output of such a process?

    A. Database

    B. Abstraction

    C. Frame

    D. Datagram

28. Which one of the following statements is false?

    A. A computer virus is a malicious program that attaches itself to files.

    B. Worms are self-replicating.

    C. Worms require human intervention for replication.

    D. A Trojan horse hides its identity.

29. In an organization, surveillance monitors such as Closed-circuit television (CCTV) are used in critical areas to monitor movement of personnel. Which of the following additional controls will not complement such a monitoring activity?

    A. A motion sensor

    B. A heat sensor

    C. An intrusion detection system

    D. A firewall

30. An organization has a security administrator and a system administrator in its rolls. Which one of the following is not a responsibility of a system administrator?

    A. Maintaining and monitoring IT assets

    B. User management

    C. Ensuring availability of IT assets

    D. Managing security configuration settings for access control

31. An organization is planning to set up a data center that houses critical business application servers. Which one of the following will be the least important factor to consider?

    A. The location is not in close proximity to toxic chemical installations.

    B. The location is not in a seismic zone.

    C. The location is not very close to seashore.

    D. The location is not very close to a metropolis.

32. In cryptography, encrypting a decrypted message results in _____.

    A. A scrambled message

    B. A decrypted message

    C. A plain text

    D. An algorithm

33. In Trusted Computing Base (TCB), a trusted shell is _____.

    A. A communication path

    B. Used by users and administrators to run trusted programs

    C. Used to check the consistency of trusted files

    D. A system that has a well-defined security policy

34. Which one of the following is FALSE pertaining to the Bell-LaPadula model?

    A. Data confidentiality model

    B. No read up

    C. No read down

    D. No write down

35. The prominent application of a Fiber Channel Protocol includes _____.

    A. IPSec

    B. Storage Area Network

    C. Hyper Text Transfer Protocol

    D. File transfer

36. Which one of the following choices is not a true statement pertaining to cryptographic algorithms?

    A. Encryption and decryption are based on algorithms.

    B. An algorithm is known as a cipher.

    C. An algorithm is a series of well-defined steps.

    D. An algorithm defines the procedure for encryption and decryption.

37. Which one of the following disaster recovery tests is also known as functional drill?

    A. Checklist review

    B. Table top exercise

    C. Simulation test

    D. Parallel test

38. A steady interference of electrical power is known as noise. What is the term used for an electrical power interference of short duration?

    A. Sag

    B. Spike

    C. Transient

    D. Inrush

39. A malicious code that tracks user actions is known as _____.

    A. Botware

    B. Worm

    C. Spyware

    D. Virus

40. Which of the following statements about the Biba model is FALSE?

    A. Data integrity model

    B. No read up

    C. No read down

    D. No write up

41. One of the most common vulnerabilities in a server using Simple Network Management Protocol based system is _____.

    A. Packet sniffing

    B. Sensitive information disclosure

    C. IP spoofing

    D. Using default community strings

42. Which one of the water sprinkler systems is the most appropriate when large volumes of water should be discharged to contain a fire?

    A. Dry pipe

    B. Wet pipe

    C. Deluge

    D. Preaction

43. One of the popular methods to authenticate the sender using sender's public key is known as _____.

    A. Public key cryptography

    B. Digital certificate

    C. Digital signature

    D. Non-repudiation

44. Which one of the following is not a true statement for information security controls?

    A. Management sets top-level information security policy.

    B. Procedural controls are detailed procedures to support policies.

    C. Management sets up technical controls.

    D. Administrative controls include monitoring activities.

45. Which one of the following is not a Denial-of-service (DoS) attack?

    A. Teardrop

    B. Smurf

    C. SYN

    D. Sniffing

46. Which one of the following choices is not a definition of risk?

    A. Risk is an exposure to a chance of loss or damage.

    B. Risk is a function of probability and consequence.

    C. Risk is a source of danger.

    D. Risk is an event that exploits vulnerabilities in systems.

47. The charge difference between neutral, hot, and ground electrical wires is known as _____.

    A. Electromatic Interference

    B. Electromechanical interference

    C. Radio Frequency Interference

    D. Electromagnetic Interference

48. Residual risk is the risk that remains after

    A. Implementation of control

    B. Control selection

    C. Risk assessment

    D. An incident

49. In web applications, a lack of verification mechanism to ensure that the sender of a web request actually intended to do so is exploited by which one of following attack?

    A. Cross-site scripting

    B. Cross-site request forgery

    C. Buffer overflow

    D. Path traversal

50. An asset is valued at $50,00,000 and it is estimated that a certain threat has the Annualized Rate of Occurrence (ARO) of once every three years. The asset is having an exposure factor (EF) of 15%. What is the highest amount a company should spend annually on countermeasures?

   A. $250,000

   B. $350,000

   C. $960,000

   D. $450,000

51. Which one of the following is not an evaluation parameter in the Information Technology Security Evaluation Criteria (ITSEC)?

   A. Functionality classes

   B. Assurance levels

   C. Correctness levels

   D. Security devices

52. The activities of a logged-in user are monitored and updated to an access log file. This process is known as _____.

   A. Authentication

   B. Audit trail

   C. Accountability

   D. Access control

53. Which one of the following is NOT a false representation of the protection domain in a Trusted Computer System (TCS)?

   A. It is a function to control or prevent direct access by an insecure, or lower-level entity, to a secure, or higher-level entity.

   B. It is a function to control or prevent direct access by an insecure, or higher-level entity, to a secure, or higher-level entity.

   C. It is a function to control or prevent direct access by an insecure, or higher-level entity, to a secure, or lower-level entity.

   D. It is a function to control or prevent direct access by an insecure, or lower-level entity, to a insecure, or higher-level entity.

54. Providing invalid or out-of-bound inputs to the database system to obtain either database access, or to obtain the database contents using the native language of the database system constitutes a type of attack known as _____.

    A. Database manipulation

    B. Denial of Service

    C. SQL Injection

    D. Arbitrary code injection

55. Which one of the following is not a threat to physical security?

    A. Theft

    B. Humidity

    C. Lack of security guard

    D. Fire

56. A high-rise wall in the physical perimeter is a physical security control. Which one of the following is a false statement for such a control?

    A. It is preventative physical control.

    B. It is a deterrent physical control.

    C. It is corrective physical control.

    D. It is a control to prevent physical intrusion.

57. If periodic port scanning is not performed on the information systems, then there is a risk of _____ created by malicious programs.

    A. Port forwarding

    B. Port mapping

    C. Turnstile doors

    D. Backdoors

58. Business Continuity Planning lifecycle includes maintenance of plans. Which one of the following choices may not provide necessary inputs for updating the plans pertaining to information security?

    A. Incidents

    B. Results of periodic risk assessments

    C. Changes to business environment

    D. Changes in tax structure

59. Trusted Computing Base (TCB) encompasses protection mechanisms that include _____.

    A. Hardware

    B. Software

    C. Firmware

    D. All of the above

60. Estimate the Single Loss Expectancy (SLE) of an asset having an Asset Value (AV) of 2000 and the Exposure Factor (EV) of 10%?

    A. 100

    B. 200

    C. 300

    D. 2000

61. A malicious activity of changing data during the input or processing stage of a software program to obtain a financial gain is known as _____.

    A. Data diddling

    B. Salami slicing

    C. Penny shaving

    D. Hacking

62. Hiding or showing menus in an application depending on the access permissions of a user is known as _____.

    A. Context-dependent access control

    B. Content-dependent access control

    C. Mandatory access control

    D. Role-based access control

63. Which one of the following is a true statement pertaining to information security procedures?

    A. Procedures support acceptable methods to implement a policy.

    B. Procedures are reference points.

    C. Procedures are high-level statements.

    D. Procedures are step-by-step instructions to implement a policy.

64. Which one of the following is not a primary memory in a computer system?

    A. Cache

    B. Hard disk

    C. Random Access Memory

    D. Read-Only Memory

65. In a Trusted Computer System (TCS), which one of the following is a security mechanism that controls the communication between entities that are labeled as low sensitive and high sensitive?

    A. Security label

    B. Logical Security Guard

    C. Protection ring

    D. Security mode

66. Which one of the following groups represents the core functions of an access control mechanism?

    A. Identification, Authorization, and Audit trail

    B. Authentication, Audit, and Accountability

    C. Authentication, Authorization, and Accountability

    D. Identification, Authorization, and Accountability

67. Which one of the following is not an assurance aim of the Public Key Infrastructure (PKI)?

    A. Confidentiality

    B. Integrity

    C. Non-repudiation

    D. Availability

68. The process of checking and validating the effectiveness of physical security controls is known as _____.

    A. Administration

    B. Assessment

    C. Auditing

    D. Analysis

69. Federal Information Processing Standard (FIPS) 140 Security Level 3 does not emphasize on _____.

    A. High probability of detection of physical attacks

    B. Response mechanisms for physical attacks

    C. Identity-based authentication

    D. Control on environmental conditions such as temperature, heat, and voltage

70. A law developed on the basis of the decisions of courts and tribunals is known as _____.

    A. Civil law

    B. Common law

    C. Religious law

    D. Statute law

71. In the Trusted Computer Security Evaluation Criteria (TCSEC), the level D signifies _____.

    A. Discretionary protection

    B. Minimal protection

    C. Mandatory protection

    D. Verified protection

72. Which one of the following is a false statement pertaining to the Take-Grant model?

    A. Take rule—a subject takes rights from another subject

    B. Grant rule—a subject grants rights to another subject

    C. Create rule—a subject creates new nodes

    D. Restore rule—a subject restores its rights over an object

73. Secret Key Cryptography is denoted as _____.

    A. Asymmetric key encryption

    B. Symmetric key encryption

    C. Public Key Cryptography

    D. Private Key Cryptography

74. Providing wrong inputs to the system can be classified as _____.

    A. A problem

    B. A vulnerability

    C. An incident

    D. A threat

75. The purpose of using Secure Shell (SSH) over Telnet is _____.

    A. SSH provides shell access to the target system

    B. SSH is faster than Telnet

    C. SSH encrypts the session and Telnet does not encrypt the session

    D. SSH is less expensive than Telnet

76. Domain Name System (DNS) maintains records to resolve host names to IP addresses. For faster resolving of addresses, web browsers store the resolved IP addresses in temporary location. Which of the following attack could most likely compromise such a mechanism to redirect user request to illegitimate addresses?

    A. Spoofing

    B. Sniffing

    C. Cache poisoning

    D. Request forging

77. Which one of the following is not an incident?

    A. System malfunction

    B. Human errors

    C. Software script execution

    D. Software malfunction

78. In a computer system, which one of the following methods attempts to reduce the time cycle to process information by overlapping fetch, decode, and execute cycles?

    A. Caching

    B. Prefetching

    C. Pipelining

    D. Encoding

79. In cryptography, if a corresponding ciphertext to the block of plaintext selected by the analyst is available, then which type of attack is possible?

    A. Ciphertext-only attack

    B. Adaptive-chosen-plaintext attack

    C. Chosen-plaintext attack

    D. Known-plaintext attack

80. When a threat event exploits a vulnerability, it results in

    A. Security measure

    B. Security improvement

    C. Security violation

    D. Security process

81. Vulnerabilities in IT systems are due to improper design, or coding, or a combination of both. Which one of the following statements is not true for vulnerabilities?

    A. Vulnerabilities are holes, or errors, in the IT systems.

    B. Vulnerabilities are exploitable by threat agents.

    C. Vulnerabilities are not exploitable.

    D. Vulnerability exploitation results in security violation.

82. In the Department of Defense Information Technology Security Certification and Accreditation Process (DITSCAP), based on which of the following specifications does document certification and accreditation take place?

    A. System Security Authorization Agreement (SSAA)

    B. System Security Auditing Agreement (SSAA)

    C. System Security Accreditation Agreement (SSAA)

    D. Security System Security Authorization Agreement (SSSAA)

83. When a sender wants to ensure that the message is not altered during transmission, the sender would use a hash function. The hash value is known as _____.

    A. Hash digest

    B. Checksum

    C. Message digest

    D. Message code

84. A type of attack that is used to listen to the communication between a client and server in a surreptitious manner is known as _____.

   A. Eavesdropping

   B. Eaveslistening

   C. Snooping

   D. Split tunneling

85. A cryptovariable is a _____.

   A. Cryptographic key

   B. Cryptographic method

   C. Cryptographic text

   D. Cryptography type

86. Which one of the following is not a type of sensor used in wave pattern motion detectors?

   A. Infrared

   B. Shortwave

   C. Microwave

   D. Ultrasonic

87. An organization has identified risks to its web servers from hacking attacks through the Internet. Which one of the following may not be a correct strategy to mitigate the risks?

   A. Establishing controls to filter the traffic to the server

   B. Establishing countermeasures in case of an unauthorized breach to the server

   C. Establishing safeguards to protect the information in the server

   D. Relocating the server to a different data centre

88. Which of the following is not true for gas discharge fire extinguishing systems?

   A. They use carbon dioxide.

   B. They are used under the floor in data centres.

   C. They use water.

   D. They use halon.

89. While doing risk assessment for physical and environmental security requirements, which one of the following will a security professional take into consideration?

    A. Physical facility

    B. Geographic operating location

    C. Supporting facilities

    D. Communications systems

90. Which one of the following statements is false pertaining to RC4 algorithm?

    A. It uses 40 to 256 bits.

    B. Key sizes are different.

    C. It is used in less complex hardware.

    D. It cannot be used for faster processing environments.

91. Which one of the following is not a risk mitigation strategy?

    A. Risk exposure

    B. Risk transfer

    C. Risk avoidance

    D. Risk acceptance

92. In a digital signature, the process of signing is accomplished by _____.

    A. Applying sender's private key to the document

    B. Applying sender's public key to the document

    C. Applying hash function

    D. Applying sender's private key to the message digest

93. The man-in-the-middle attack is an example of _____.

    A. Sniffing

    B. Spoofing

    C. Eavesdropping

    D. Cache poisoning

94. At what temperature is the valve of wet pipe sprinkling system designed to open?

    A. 164o Fahrenheit

    B. 164o Celsius

    C. 165o Celsius

    D. 165o Fahrenheit

95. Which one of the following is not a primary objective of the Orange book?

    A. Accountability

    B. Assurance

    C. Policy

    D. Authentication

96. Which algorithm is used by Pretty Good Privacy (PGP)?

    A. Triple-DES

    B. Twofish

    C. International Data Encryption Algorithm (IDEA)

    D. Blowfish

97. IEEE 802.11 is a set of standards for which of the following types of networking technologies?

    A. Wireless Local Area Networking (WLAN)

    B. Local Area Networking (LAN)

    C. Wide Area Networking (WAN)

    D. Metropolitan Area Networking (MAN)

98. Which one of the following does not determine the strength or security of a cryptographic key?

    A. Length of the key

    B. Entropy

    C. Quality of encryption algorithm

    D. Initialization vectors

99. Which one of the following is not true in an access control environment?

    A. A subject sets access control restrictions to an object.

    B. A subject seeks to access an object.

    C. A subject controls the access.

    D. A subject is a physical equipment.

100. Which one of the following choices is correct for Annualized Loss Expectancy (ALE)?

    A. Single Loss Expectancy divided by Annual Rate of Occurrence

    B. Asset Value multiplied by Exposure Factor

    C. Asset Value multiplied by Annual Rate of Occurrence

    D. Single Loss Expectancy multiplied by Annual Rate of Occurrence

101. Which one of the following is not true pertaining to Grey box penetration testing?

   A. The scope of testing can be from external or internal networks.

   B. While testing from external networks, the details of internal network are not known to the tester.

   C. While testing from external networks, the details of internal network are known to the tester.

   D. While testing from internal network, the details of the network are not known to the tester.

102. The address pace of IPv6 is _____.

   A. 216 IP addresses

   B. 2128 IP addresses

   C. 264 IP addresses

   D. 232 IP addresses

103. Which one of the following is not a primary purpose of cryptography?

   A. Concealing confidential information from unauthorized users

   B. Ensuring immediate detection of any alteration made to the concealed information

   C. Ensuring availability of confidential information all the time

   D. Converting a plaintext to a ciphertext

104. A cold boot attack is used to retrieve information, such as password or encryption keys, from the DRAM memories even after the power is removed. Which property of DRAM memories is this attack trying to compromise?

   A. Data Retention

   B. Data Emanation

   C. Data Remanence

   D. Data Encryption

105. Which one of the following is not a phase in system security life cycle?

   A. Integration phase

   B. Initiation phase

   C. Implementation phase

   D. Disposal phase

106. An exposure factor can be best described as _____.

    A. The rate of occurrence of a threat event

    B. Measure of an impact

    C. Measure of a vulnerability

    D. Measure of risk

107. While developing the business continuity plans, which of the following should be considered as a most important requirement?

    A. Confidentiality

    B. Integrity

    C. Availability

    D. Business plans

108. In physical security, guards and dogs are controls that are used to prevent, detect, deter, and react to an intrusion event. Which one of the following is not true for such forms of controls?

    A. Guards are better suited in adapting to situations.

    B. Guards are more expensive form of control than dogs.

    C. Dogs are suitable for reactive actions based on judgement.

    D. Dogs are suitable in hostile environment that do not support human intervention.

109. Replay attacks are due to improper handling of _____.

    A. Authentication process

    B. Session data

    C. Application inputs

    D. Boundary values

110. Sending Unsolicited Commercial Email (UCE) is popularly known as _____.

    A. Phishing

    B. Pharming

    C. SmiShing

    D. Spamming

111. Which one of the following is not an asset classification criterion?

   A. Age

   B. Useful degree

   C. Useful life

   D. Value

112. A turnstile type of fencing should be considered in which of the following situations?

   A. When a group of people can be allowed at a time through the gate

   B. When a man-trap system is required

   C. When a single person should be allowed to pass through the gate at a time

   D. When intrusion detection systems are installed

113. For proper operation of computer parts, the ideal humidity range should be 40 and 60%. What type of problem will occur if the humidity is above 60%?

   A. Electric plating

   B. Electro plating

   C. Condensation

   D. Static electricity

114. Threats exploit vulnerabilities through their _____.

   A. Associates

   B. Adversaries

   C. Agents

   D. Angles

115. At what phase of System Development Life Cycle should sensitive assessment be conducted?

   A. Acquisition phase

   B. Initiation phase

   C. Disposal phase

   D. Operation phase

116. Which one of the following is not an intellectual property?

    A. Copyright

    B. Patent

    C. Trademark

    D. Trading

117. Which one of the following is not a disadvantage of having 6' to 7' fencing?

    A. It is too easy to climb.

    B. It deters most intruders.

    C. It deters a casual trespasser.

    D. It can be used in internal boundaries.

118. Which one of the following is not a Class C combustible material?

    A. Paper

    B. Energised electrical equipments

    C. Flammable chemicals

    D. Soda acid

119. A strong session management prevents what type of attack?

    A. Sniffing

    B. Spoofing

    C. Hijacking

    D. SYN

120. Which of the following statements pertaining to a security policy is incorrect?

    A. It emphasizes the role of system owners and administrators in protecting technology and information assets.

    B. It specifies how computer systems should be used using a specific technology.

    C. It shows management commitment and direction for information security.

    D. It must be reviewed periodically.

121. Which of the following is not a true choice for Kerberos implementation?

    A. It can be used to authenticate network services

    B. It can be used to provide third-party verification services

    C. It maintains a centralized server

    D. Kerberos server is a single point of compromise

122. When a plaintext is Exclusively-ORed (XORed) with the previous block of ciphertext, then the mode is known as _____.

    A. Electronic Code Block

    B. Electronic Code Book

    C. Cipher Block Chaining

    D. Cipher Feedback

123. Basic Input Output System (BIOS) checks can be used to control access to the system using password protection. This control is known as _____.

    A. Pre-boot authorization

    B. Pre-boot authentication

    C. Boot sector authentication

    D. Pre-boot identification

124. Which of the following information security models proposes a directed graph?

    A. The Biba model

    B. The Clark-Wilson model

    C. The Take-Grant model

    D. The Integrity model

125. When a malicious code that came disguised inside a trusted program gets activated on a particular event or date, then such malicious code is known as

    A. Trojan horse

    B. Malware

    C. Logic Bomb

    D. Virus

126. Which one of the following choice is false with respect to Common Criteria (CC)?

    A. It is an assurance framework

    B. It defines protection profile

    C. The standard ISO/IEC 15408 is based on Common Criteria (CC)

    D. The standard ISO/IEC 27001 is based on Common Criteria (CC)

127. An access card that contains integrated circuits and can process information for physical and logical access control is known as

    A. ATM card

    B. Credit card

    C. Supplementary card

    D. Smart card

128. Which one of the following is a correct description of a preventative control?

    A. Preventative control is to predict the occurrence of an undesirable event

    B. Preventative control is to reduce the effect of an attack

    C. Preventative control triggers a corrective control

    D. Preventative controls are to prevent security violations

129. CAPTCHA, one of the popular mechanisms used by web sites to control input to access control system is supplied by humans and not machines. This mechanism is known as Completely Automated Public Turing test to tell Computers and Humans Apart (CAPTCHA). Which type of machines that this access control system is predominantly concerned with?

    A. WebDots

    B. BotNets

    C. WebBots

    D. WebNets

130. Which one of the following is not a right consideration while designing a data center?

    A. Avoiding windows in the data centers

    B. Using raised floors to house cables and ducts

    C. Designing doors to allow air to flow inside when opened

    D. Maintain optimum temperature

131. An access control model that uses the pair of values that are related to least upper bound and the greatest lower bound in a model is known as _____.

    A. Discretionary access control

    B. Non-discretionary access control

    C. Matrix based access control

    D. Lattice based access control

132. Which of the following document in Common Criteria contain Security Functions Requirement (SFR)?

    A. Target of Evaluation

    B. Security target

    C. Evaluation Assurance level

    D. Target of Evolution

133. Secret and hidden channels that transmit information to unauthorized entities based on the response time of the system is known as _____.

    A. Covert storage channel

    B. Covert channel

    C. Covert timing channel

    D. Covert information channel

134. Secure Sockets Layer (SSL) is a popular protocol that uses cryptographic encryption to protect the communication data. Which type of cipher this protocol uses for such protection?

    A. Block cipher

    B. Stream cipher

    C. Triple-DES

    D. Rijndael algorithm

135. Which one of the following statements pertaining to combustible materials is false?

    A. Cloth and rubber are Class A materials

    B. Magnesium and sodium are Class D materials

    C. Oils and Greases are Class B materials

    D. Water is a Class C material

136. The focus of red book in rainbow series published by US Department of Defense (DoD) is _____.

   A. Integrity

   B. Confidentiality

   C. Authenticity

   D. Confidentiality and Integrity

137. Which one the following is not a true statement pertaining to the parameter that indicates the Mean Time Between Failure (MTBF) of devices?

   A. MTBF is a time measurement that specifies an average time between failures

   B. MTBF is known as the useful life of the device

   C. MTBF is the average time required to repair the device

   D. Higher MTBF means more reliable device

138. Which one of the following pertaining to Fire suppression medium is false?

   A. Halon is a fire suppression medium

   B. Halon is very widely used fire suppression medium

   C. Halon is a Ozone-depleting substance

   D. Halon is no longer allowed to be used as a fire suppression medium

139. Which one of the following method is most suitable for protecting copyrighted information?

   A. Steganography

   B. Digital watermarking

   C. SecureID

   D. Digital signature

140. Which of the following information security model is also known as a State machine model?

   A. The Take-Grant model

   B. The Bell-LaPadula model

   C. The Biba Model

   D. The Clark-Wilson model

141. Which of the following is not a cyber crime?

    A. Cyberterrorism

    B. Denial-of-service attacks

    C. Spamming

    D. Online shopping

142. The systematic use of information to identify sources and to estimate the risk is known as _____.

    A. Risk evaluation

    B. Risk treatment

    C. Risk acceptance

    D. Risk analysis

143. When you want to ensure that the message that you send can be opened only by the receiver, then you will _____.

    A. Encrypt the document using your public key

    B. Encrypt the document using receivers private key

    C. Encrypt the document using your private key

    D. Encrypt the document using receivers public key

144. Potable fire extinguishers predominantly use which fire suppression medium?

    A. Halon

    B. Carbon dioxide (CO_2)

    C. Water

    D. Magnesium

145. An Artificial Intelligence system that tries to mimic the processing ability of human brain is known as

    A. Expert system

    B. Brain mapping

    C. Neural network

    D. Speech recognition

146. Which one of the following is NOT an ideal choice when an organization needs to resume their critical IT operations in 24 to 48 hours?

A. Cold Site

B. Warm Site

C. Hot Site

D. Data site

147. The amount of time or effort required to accomplish an attack is known as _____.

A. Work load

B. Attack vector

C. Work factor

D. Attack factor

148. The layer that manages the communication between two computers in OSI model is the

A. Network layer

B. Session layer

C. Data link layer

D. Application layer

149. Fooling an information system to make it trust an entity that has imitated the trusted entity is known as

A. Sniffing

B. Social engineering

C. Smurf

D. Spoofing

150. Which one of the following control will be most effective to prevent data theft due to data remanence in the storage media?

A. Degaussing

B. Formatting seven times

C. Physically destroying the media

D. Erasing the data before reuse

151. Hash value in cryptography is computed value based on the contents of the message. What is this computed value called?

    A. Primesum

    B. Key strength

    C. Checksum

    D. One-way function

152. If an access to an asset is determined by its owner, then such an access control is termed as _____.

    A. Mandatory

    B. Rule based

    C. Discretionary

    D. Lattice based

153. Which one of the following is a service asset?

    A. Computer

    B. Air Conditioner

    C. Printer

    D. Computing

154. Which one of the following is false pertaining to information owners?

    A. Owners are entrusted with day-to-day maintenance of information

    B. Owners delegate the maintenance of information to the custodian

    C. Owners determine the classification level of the information

    D. Owners are responsible for the protection of the information

155. An organization is doing risk assessment for the Information Technology department. Which one of the following choice would not yield much input for the assessment?

    A. Classification of assets

    B. List of threats

    C. Vulnerability assessment reports

    D. Number of audits

156. Which one of the following protocols is most likely to reduce the manual configuration of IP addresses to host computers?

    A. Transmission control protocol

    B. Internet protocol

    C. Dynamic Host Control Protocol

    D. Address Resolution Protocol

157. IPsec is a set of protocols that are used to secure Internet communications. Which of the following is not a key function of the protocol?

    A. Authentication

    B. Encryption

    C. Key exchange

    D. Key modification

158. Randomization vulnerabilities are predominantly concerned with _____.

    A. Access control

    B. Encryption

    C. Authentication

    D. Boundary condition

159. Providing Personnel Identification Number (PIN) along with a smart card and swiping a finger constitutes what type of authentication?

    A. Multi-tier

    B. Two-factor

    C. Three-factor

    D. Factoring

160. In Cryptography, when key is authorized for use by legitimate entries for a period of time, then such a period is known as _____.

    A. Cryptovariable

    B. Cryptotime

    C. Cryptoperiod

    D. Cryptanalysis

161. Which one of the following is not true pertaining to Virtual Private Networking (VPN)?

   A. VPN is a virtual network within a public network such as Internet

   B. VPN uses the concept of tunneling

   C. A tunnel in VPN is an unencrypted path

   D. VPN uses IPSec protocols

162. In the Bell-LaPadula model, which one of the following statements is false?

   A. The security properties are related to the Mandatory Access Control and Discretionary Access Control.

   B. The model prescribes access controls to classified or confidential information.

   C. The security properties related to the Mandatory Access Control and Non-Discretionary Access Control.

   D. The focus of the model is confidentiality.

163. Which one of the following choice in an audit trail is unlikely to contain in the access log file pertaining to physical access?

   A. Access attempts

   B. Access results such as success or failure

   C. Locations accessed

   D. Access control list

164. Which one of the following is false pertaining to the TCP/IP protocols?

   A. TCP is a connection oriented protocol where as UDP is a connectionless protocol.

   B. TCP is a connectionless protocol whereas IP is a connection oriented protocol.

   C. Internet protocol works in the Internet layer of the TCP/IP model.

   D. TCP works in the transport layer of the TCP/IP model.

165. The concept of least privilege is applicable to _____.

   A. System administrators

   B. Security administrators

   C. Users

   D. Operators

166. In the Orange book, audit trails is a form of _____.

    A. Controlled access protection

    B. Minimal protection

    C. Structured protection

    D. Verified protection

167. Border Gateway Protocols works in which layer of the TCP/IP model?

    A. Application layer

    B. Physical layer

    C. Data link layer

    D. Transport layer

168. Patch management is a systematic way of applying the patches to the applications. Which one of the following is not a right action while applying patches?

    A. Applying patches in the test environment

    B. Creating roll-back mechanisms

    C. Applying patches directly to production systems

    D. Documenting the patch and configuration changes

169. Which one of the following statements is false?

    A. A computer virus is a malicious program that attaches itself to files.

    B. Worms are self-replicating.

    C. Worms require human intervention for replication.

    D. A Trojan horse hides its identity.

170. Which one of the following software development life cycle frameworks emphasizes on iteration throughout the development life cycle?

    A. Agile framework

    B. Spiral model

    C. Incremental model

    D. Waterfall model

171. In Public Key Infrastructure, which of the following is not a key management procedure?

    A. Secure Storage of Keys

    B. Secure Distribution of Keys

    C. Secure Destruction of Keys

    D. Secure Modification of Keys

172. Asymmetric key encryption is also known as _____.

    A. Private Key Cryptography

    B. Private Key Encryption

    C. Public Key Cryptography

    D. Public Key Infrastructure

173. An armed response to intrusion is a _____.

    A. Preventive-administrative control

    B. Preventive-technical control

    C. Reactive-physical control

    D. Reactive-administrative control

174. An organization is planning to conduct information security awareness training programs to its employees. Which one of the following topic should they consider and emphasize as the most important?

    A. Briefing the security requirements of the organization

    B. Legal responsibilities of the organization

    C. Business controls

    D. Usage instructions that relate to information-processing facilities

175. At what stage of penetration testing, are vulnerability scanners used?

    A. Scoping

    B. Penetrating testing

    C. Information analysis planning

    D. Vulnerability detection

176. The practice of discovering the full content of a DNS zone via successive queries is known as _____.

    A. Zone transfer

    B. Zone update

    C. Zone security

    D. Zone enumeration

177. Separation of users and data is an example of which type of assurance?

    A. Operational assurance

    B. Life Cycle assurance

    C. System assurance

    D. Network assurance

178. In computer crime, the role of computer could be _____.

    A. Crime committed against a computer

    B. Crime committed using a computer

    C. Computer is incidental in the crime

    D. All of the above

179. Which one of the following is not true for Recovery Time Objectives (RTO) pertaining to Business Continuity Planning?

    A. It is a timeframe within which the systems should be recovered.

    B. It is indicated in terms of hours/days.

    C. Maximum period of time of transaction data that a business can afford to loose during successful recovery.

    D. It is based on Service Level Agreements.

180. The goal of the code of ethics by (ISC)^2 includes _____.

    A. Protecting society, the commonwealth, and the infrastructure

    B. Acting honorably, honestly, justly, responsibly, and legally

    C. Providing diligent and competent service to principals

    D. All of the above

181. Which one of the following is a crime committed by identity theft?

    A. Online purchases through stolen credit cards

    B. Selling skimmed credit cards

    C. Sending spam mails by spoofing mail addresses

    D. Breaking into the bank and stealing money

182. Which one of the following attacks does not represent a form of social engineering?

    A. Phishing

    B. 419 Nigerian spam

    C. Denial of Service

    D. Trojan horse

183. Keyloggers capture the keystrokes of an unsuspicious user. Which one of the following attacks represents a behavior that may be capturing the activity information in the network?

    A. Spamming

    B. Sniffing

    C. Replay attacks

    D. Pinging

184. Which one of the following is not a right choice pertaining the criminal law?

    A. It deals with the violations of the government laws

    B. Criminal laws are files by government agencies against an individual or an organization

    C. It deals with lawsuit files by private parties such as individuals and corporations

    D. The punishment under criminal law includes imprisonment

185. _____ is a set of exclusive rights granted to the inventor of new, useful, inventive, and industry-applications.

    A. Copyright

    B. Patent

    C. Trademark

    D. Trade secret

186. Sarbanes-Oxley mandates a number of reforms to _____.

    A. Enhance corporate responsibility

    B. Financial disclosures

    C. Combat corporate and accounting fraud

    D. All of the above

187. Which one of the following statement pertaining to communication protocol is false?

   A. A protocol is a communication standard.

   B. A protocol is a network traffic routing device.

   C. A protocol defines rules pertaining to syntax and semantics.

   D. A protocol defines rules pertaining to synchronization for communications.

188. The upper four layers in the OSI model are sometimes referred as_____

   A. Network layers

   B. Media layer

   C. Host layers

   D. Communication layers

189. Spoofing can also be referred to as _____.

   A. Masquerading

   B. Disguising

   C. Impersonating

   D. All of the above

190. Which of the following is not a service provided by the Domain Name System Security Extensions (DNSSEC)?

   A. Authentication

   B. Accounting

   C. Data integrity

   D. Authenticated Denial of Existence

191. Which one of the following statements pertaining to Dynamic Host Control Protocol (DHCP) is false?

   A. DHCP uses Point-to-Point Protocol (PPP).

   B. DHCP uses Network Address Translation (NAT) for assigning IP addresses.

   C. DHCP is preferred method of IP allocation to routers and firewalls.

   D. The address allocation method is termed as Request, Offer, Send, Accept (ROSA).

192. Path traversal is a type of attack that tries to _____.

    A. Compromise availability of a server

    B. Spoof the network traffic

    C. Gain unauthorized access to web server directory structure

    D. Corrupt the database

193. Which one of the following cryptographic standards uses three 56-bit keys?

    A. Data Encryption Standard

    B. Triple-DES

    C. Advanced Encryption Standard

    D. Blowfish

194. Secure Electronic Transaction (SET) is a _____.

    A. Set of standard protocols for file transfer

    B. Set of standard protocols for web browsing

    C. Set of standard protocols for securing credit card transactions over insecure networks

    D. None of the above

195. What is the normal range of a raised floor in a data center?

    A. 2 to 3 feet

    B. 2 to 4 meters

    C. 300 to 800mm

    D. 50 to 90cm

196. The periodical mock tests rehearsing the steps of actions to be taken during an emergency are also known as _____.

    A. Table top review

    B. Evacuation drills

    C. Fire fighting

    D. Shutdown of systems

197. Full disk encryption is used to encrypt the data in laptops. This is to prevent which type of attack?

    A. Warm boot attack

    B. Hot boot attack

    C. Cold boot attack

    D. Boot sector attack

198. The average time required to repair a device is termed as _____.

    A. Mean Time Between Failure

    B. Useful life of device

    C. Mean Time To Repair

    D. Mean Time to Install

199. Which one of the following is a method of destroying data in a magnetic media?

    A. Delinking

    B. Degaussing

    C. Deguessing

    D. Debuffering

200. In trusted computing, protection domains are organized in hierarchical format. They are known as

    A. Protection domain

    B. Security perimeter

    C. Protection rings

    D. Protection path

201. A technique to hide information from unauthorized entities is known as _____.

    A. Reference monitor

    B. Salami slicing

    C. Encapsulation

    D. Emanation

202. How many Evaluation Assurance Levels (EAL) are defined in Common Criteria?

    A. 3

    B. 9

    C. 8

    D. 7

203. System Security Engineering—Capability Maturity Model defines two sets of security processes. One is Security Engineering Practices, choose the other.

A. Security management processes

B. Security organizational processes

C. Security administrative processes

D. Security technical processes

204. *-property states that a subject at a given security level may not write to any object at a lower security level. Which security model states this property?

A. The Bell-LaPadula Model

B. The Take-Grant model

C. The Biba model

D. The Clark-Wilson model

205. In Biometrics, identification provided by a person is verified by a process known as one-to-one search. This process can be described as _____.

A. Authorization

B. Identification

C. Authentication

D. Access control

206. An authority that manages the certificates in a Public Key Infrastructure is known as _____.

A. Root authority

B. System authority

C. Certification authority

D. Digital authority

207. The Rijndael encryption algorithm uses key sizes up to _____.

A. 32 bits

B. 1024 bits

C. 512 bits

D. 256 bits

208. Which one of the following algorithms is not useful for hashing?

    A. MD4

    B. MD5

    C. MD2

    D. RC4

209. Kerberos is more suitable for preventing _____.

    A. Spoofing attacks

    B. Replay attacks

    C. Phishing attacks

    D. Decryption attacks

210. Information security best practices, termed as code of practices, are covered by which of the following standards?

    A. ISO/IEC 27001

    B. ISO/IEC 9001

    C. ISO/IEC 27002

    D. Common Criteria

211. In the Orange Book, mandatory protection is required in the following levels _____.

    A. B and D

    B. A and C

    C. A and B

    D. B and C

212. The disposal phase in system development life cycle is concerned with _____.

    A. Disposition of information

    B. Disposition of hardware and software

    C. Disposition of media

    D. All of the above

213. In software development life cycle, verification during development and implementation is a process to check _____.

    A. Adherence to timelines

    B. Adherence to budgets

    C. Adherence to software specifications.

    D. Adherence to hardware specifications

214. What is the biggest concern in using a waterfall model for software development?

    A. It is a top to bottom approach

    B. It is a simplistic approach

    C. The activities have to be completed in sequence

    D. The approach does not support rework

215. Which of the following is a core security consideration for secure software development processes?

    A. User authentication

    B. Password management

    C. Access controls

    D. All of the above

216. From security perspective, which one of the following procedures is the most important during software development processes?

    A. Hardware configuration procedure

    B. Network setup procedure

    C. Change control procedure

    D. Documentation procedure

217. In object-oriented programming, treating derived class members just like their parent class members is known as _____.

    A. Encapsulation

    B. Abstraction

    C. Polymorphism

    D. Method

218. An Artificial Intelligence system tries to mimic human brains primarily in the _____.

  A. Numerical ability

  B. Linguistic ability

  C. Perception and decision-making

  D. All of the above

219. Failure to properly create, store, transmit, or protect password is an example of _____.

  A. Improper network management

  B. Insufficient access controls

  C. Improper credentials management

  D. Insufficient authentication mechanisms

220. Failure of a web application to validate, filter, or encode user input before returning it to another user's web client is known as _____.

  A. Path traversal

  B. Cross-site scripting

  C. Cross-site request forgery

  D. Input validation

221. Mobile codes are executed in _____.

  A. Server

  B. Target machine

  C. Network

  D. Routers

222. Which one of the following is a common data structure attack?

  A. Altering the data in primary memory

  B. Rearranging the order of execution in the memory

  C. Malicious code execution through data buffer

  D. All of the above

223. Encryption of data between client and the server in an Internet web browsing session and it can be accomplished using _____.

   A. SSL

   B. HTTP

   C. FTP

   D. DHCP

224. Which one of the following is not a technical control?

   A. Firewall

   B. Security policy

   C. Intrusion Detection Systems

   D. Anti-virus software

225. An organization's security initiatives based on policies, procedures, and guidelines; security awareness training; and risk management together defines the _____.

   A. Security setup

   B. Security posture

   C. Security management

   D. Security initiative

226. Which one of the following parameters is considered for assets during asset classification that helps in devising suitable controls for security protection?

   A. Value

   B. Sensitivity

   C. Degree of assurance required

   D. All of the above

227. Which one of the following classification of information, if compromised, could cause certain damage to national security as per governmental classification types?

   A. Top secret

   B. Secret

   C. Confidential

   D. Sensitive but unclassified

228. Which one of the following is the highest level of classification in private sectors pertaining to information assets?

    A. Public

    B. Sensitive

    C. Private

    D. Confidential

229. While initiating Business Continuity Planning process, which of the following is first established?

    A. Roles and responsibilities

    B. Alternative sites

    C. Testing the plans

    D. Performing the impact analysis

230. Business continuity plan should identify _____.

    A. Mission critical systems

    B. Business impact due to non-availability of critical systems

    C. Preventive and recovery controls

    D. All of the above

231. A call tree in Business Continuity Planning represents a _____.

    A. List of personnel associated with the continuity processes

    B. List of technical department personnel

    C. List of external auditors

    D. List of administrative staff

232. Which of the following is important for business continuity processes?

    A. Step-by-step procedure for recovery

    B. Appropriate testing of BC plans

    C. Awareness of people

    D. All of the above

233. Sequenced Packet eXchange (SPX) is part of which protocol suit?

    A. TCP/IP

    B. OSI

    C. SPX/IPX

    D. IPX/SPX

234. Half-open connections is a vulnerability in _____.

    A. SPX protocol

    B. HTTP

    C. TCP

    D. IP

235. SYN cookies are _____.

    A. Attacks on TCP protocol implementation

    B. Used in Spoofing

    C. Security control for SYN attacks

    D. A Denial of Service attack

236. In client server networking, cookies are _____.

    A. Text files sent by server to client

    B. A type of attack

    C. Virus

    D. A malicious code

237. The process of sending ECHO_REQUEST using Internet Control Messaging Protocol is popularly known as _____.

    A. Digging

    B. Pinging

    C. Tunneling

    D. Echoing

238. Which one of the following is the function of Network/Internet layer protocols?

    A. Passing the outgoing packets though the gateways to the next layer

    B. Passing the incoming packets to the transport layer

    C. Provide error detection and diagnostics for the incoming and outgoing packets

    D. All of the above

239. In networking, multicasting refers to _____.

    A. One-to-one communication

    B. Many-to-one communication

    C. Many-to-many communication

    D. One-to-many communication

240. Which one of the following protocol is used to obtain IP addresses based on hardware address?

   A. Address Resolution Protocol

   B. Neighbour Discovery protocol

   C. Reverse Address Resolution Protocol

   D. Point-to-Point Tunneling protocol

241. Overwriting ARP table entries with malicious address is known as _____.

   A. ARP routing

   B. ARP caching

   C. ARP poisoning

   D. ARP tunnelling

242. A momentary low voltage is _____.

   A. Sag

   B. Spike

   C. Fault

   D. Blackout

243. Water is more preferable for which class of fire?

   A. Class C

   B. Class A

   C. Class B

   D. Class D

244. Under what conditions are Class A fire extinguishers used?

   A. When the fire involves electrical equipment

   B. When the fire involves paper

   C. When fire is due to oils

   D. When the fire is due to flammable chemicals

245. Using cameras to monitor the critical areas is a _____.

   A. Preventive control

   B. Deterrent control

   C. Detective control

   D. Corrective control

246. When multiple CPUs are used to process information, the process is known as _____.

   A. Multitasking

   B. Multithreading

   C. Multiprocessing

   D. Multimedia

247. Which one of the following is the least expensive alternative site for disaster recovery?

   A. Dual site

   B. Warm site

   C. Cold site

   D. Hot site

248. Which one of the following sites provides the highest redundancy?

   A. Hot site

   B. Dual site

   C. Warm site

   D. Cold site

249. Reliability of a device is more if its _____.

   A. MTBF is more and MTTR is more

   B. MTBF is more and MTTR is less

   C. MTBF is less and MTTR is more

   D. MTBF is less and MTTR is less

250. Which one of the following Intellectual Property Rights defines proprietary formulae or design that protects the information being copied and prevents competitions to gain advantage?

   A. Trademark

   B. Patent

   C. Copyright

   D. Trade secret

Answers

Question No.	Solution	Question No.	Solution	Question No.	Solution
1	D	26	B	51	D
2	B	27	D	52	C
3	C	28	C	53	A
4	D	29	D	54	C
5	C	30	D	55	C
6	C	31	D	56	C
7	A	32	A	57	D
8	D	33	B	58	D
9	A	34	C	59	D
10	B	35	B	60	B
11	A	36	B	61	A
12	C	37	D	62	B
13	B	38	C	63	D
14	B	39	C	64	B
15	D	40	B	65	B
16	A	41	D	66	C
17	A	42	C	67	D
18	D	43	A	68	C
19	A	44	C	69	D
20	C	45	D	70	B
21	A	46	D	71	B
22	C	47	D	72	D
23	A	48	A	73	B
24	D	49	B	74	C
25	A	50	A	75	C

Question No.	Solution	Question No.	Solution	Question No.	Solution
76	C	101	D	126	D
77	C	102	B	127	D
78	B	103	C	128	A
79	C	104	C	129	C
80	C	105	A	130	C
81	C	106	B	131	D
82	A	107	C	132	B
83	C	108	C	133	C
84	A	109	B	134	B
85	A	110	D	135	D
86	B	111	B	136	D
87	D	112	C	137	C
88	C	113	C	138	B
89	D	114	C	139	B
90	D	115	B	140	B
91	A	116	D	141	D
92	D	117	A	142	D
93	B	118	B	143	D
94	D	119	C	144	B
95	D	120	B	145	C
96	C	121	B	146	D
97	A	122	C	147	C
98	D	123	B	148	B
99	D	124	C	149	D
100	D	125	C	150	C

Question No.	Solution	Question No.	Solution	Question No.	Solution
151	C	176	D	201	C
152	C	177	A	202	D
153	D	178	D	203	B
154	A	179	C	204	A
155	D	180	D	205	C
156	C	181	D	206	C
157	D	182	C	207	D
158	B	183	B	208	D
159	C	184	C	209	B
160	C	185	B	210	C
161	C	186	D	211	C
162	C	187	B	212	D
163	D	188	B	213	C
164	B	189	D	214	D
165	C	190	B	215	D
166	A	191	C	216	C
167	C	192	C	217	C
168	C	193	B	218	C
169	C	194	D	219	C
170	A	195	C	220	B
171	D	196	B	221	B
172	C	197	C	222	D
173	C	198	C	223	A
174	D	199	B	224	B
175	D	200	C	225	B
226	D	235	C	244	B
227	C	236	A	245	C
228	D	237	B	246	C
229	A	238	D	247	C
230	D	239	D	248	B
231	A	240	C	249	B
232	D	241	C	250	D
233	D	242	A		
234	C	243	B		

References

1. *Official (ISC)² Guide to the CISSP CBK*, Aureback Publications.
2. *The CISSP and CAP Prep Guide: Platinum Edition*
    by Ronald L. Krutz (Author), Russell Dean Vines (Author) .
3. (ISC)² website – www.isc2.org.
4. Wikipedia – www.wikipedia.org.
5. CCCure – www.cccure.org.
6. ISO Standards – www.ISO.CH.
7. NIST standards – www.nist.gov.
8. NVD – http://nvd.nist.gov.
9. CVE – http://cve.mitre.org.

Index

Elliptic Curve Cryptography 87
Message Digest Algorithm (MAD) 88
private key 86
public key 86
Rivest, Shamir and Adleman (RSA) 87
auditing, facility security
access logs 55
audit trail 54
error logs 55
important points 54
logs 55

B

BCP
about 193, 195
and DRP, differences 202
and DRP, similarities 202
availability factor 195
goals 195
knowledge requirements 193
objective 195
practice questions 200
BCP, process
about 198
Business Impact Analysis, continuity
plan 197
Business Impact Analysis, performing 196
Business Impact Analysis, What-If scenario
used 196
contents 199
identity points 198
measures 198
plan, developing 197
plan, implementing 197
plan, testing 197
plan awareness, creating 197
plan initiation 196
plan maintenance 197
procedures 199
qualities 197
Recovery Point Objective (RPO) 198
Recovery Time Objective (RTO) 198
resources 198
scoping 196

**Bell-LaPadula model, information
security model**
*-property (star property) 190
about 190
discretionary security property 190
simple security property 190
BGP, link layer protocols
applications 172
attacks 172
countermeasures 172
layers 172
message or data injection 172
Multi Protocol Label Switching (MPLS) 172
purpose 172
threats 172
vulnerabilities 172
Biba model, information security model
* (star) Integrity Axiom 191
data integrity 191
Simple Integrity Axiom 191
black hat hacker 211
block cipher, symmetric key encryption
Advanced Encryption Standard (AES) 85
Blowfish 85
Cipher Block Chaining (CBC) 86
Cipher FeedBack (CFB) 86
Data Encryption Standard (DES) 85
Electronic Code Book (ECB) 86
examples 85
International Data Encryption Algorithm
(IDEA) 86
intialization vectors 86
Output FeedBack (OFB) 86
Triple-DES 85
Twofish 85
Border Gateway Protocol. *See* **BGP, link
layer protocols**
Business Continuity Planning. *See* **BCP**

C

**Candian Trusted Computer Product
Evaluation Criteria (CTCPEC) 186**
CAPTCHA 63
CC, assurance
about 184
concepts 185

fraud, computer crimes
about 211
data diddling 211
hacking 211
penny shaving 211
salami slicing 211
FTP, application layer protocols
about 157
applications 158
attacks 158
countermeasures 158
layers 158
Secure File Transfer Protocol (SFTP) 158
threats 158
vulnerabilities 158

G

grey hat hacker 211

H

hacker 211
Hard Disk Drives (HDD) 58
hashing, encryption types
algorithm example used 88
checksum 87
purpose 88
Health Insurance Portability and
Accountability. *See* **HIPAA, act**
HIPPA, act
about 220
privacy role 220
security role 220
HTTP, application layer protocols
applications 157
attacks 157
countermeasures 157
eavesdropping 157
layers 157
path traversal 157
Secure Hyper Text Transfer Protocol
(S-HTTP or HTTPS) 157
TCP used 156
threats 157
validation 157
vulnerabilities 157

Hyper Text Transfer Protocol. *See* **HTTP,**
application layer protocols

I

IEC 30
IEEE802.11 104
International Electrotechnical
Commission *See* **IEC 30**
IMAP, application layer protocols
about 158
applications 158
attacks 159
countermeasures 159
layer 158
threats 159
vulnerabilities 159
incident management
about 113
goals 114
incident reporting 113
incidents, examples 113, 114
objective 114
preventive actions 114
information security, computer architecture
abstraction 179
encapsulation 179
logical security guard 180
protection domain 179
protection rings 179
reference monitor 180
security kernel 180
security label 180
security modes 180
security perimeter 179
security policy 178
Trusted Computing Base (TCB) 178
Trusted Computing System (TCS) 179
trusted path 179
information security, security
management practices
accountability 21
assuring 21
authorization 21
privacy 21
purpose 15

National Institute of Standards and
    Technology. *See* **NIST**
National Vulnerability Database (NVD) 78
Network/Internet layer
  about 167
  gateways 167
Network/Internet layer, protocols
  functions 168
  IP 168
  IP sec protocols 169
network architecture
  communication 150
  communication, mediums 150
  layered architecture 151
  OSI 151
  protocols used 151
  TCP/IP 153
  telecommunication 151
NIACAP 187
NIST
  about 23, 30
  identification phase 30
  managing phase 30
  evaluating phase 30
**non-discretionary access control, access
    control**
  centralized access control 65
  de-centralized access control 66
  distributed access control 66
  lattice based access control 66
  Mandatory Access Control (MAC) 65
  Rule Based Access Control (RBAC) 65
  task based access control 65
non-repudiation 96

O

**object-oriented systems, information
    technology systems**
  about 140
  OOP 140
Object Oriented Programming. *See* **OOP,
    object-oriented systems**
OOP, object-oriented systems
  abstraction 140
  class 140
  encapsulation 140

  functions 140
  inheritance 140
  instance 140
  message passing 140
  method 140
  object 140
  Object-Oriented Analysis (OOA) 140
  Object-Oriented Design (OOD) 140
  polymorphism 140
Open System Interconnect. *See* **OSI,
    network architecture**
operations security
  about 117
  approach, in CISSP exam 110
  documented operating procedures 111
  knowledge reqirements 109
  overview 109
  practice questions 116
orange book 185
OSI, network architecture
  about 151, 153
  host layers 152
  layers 152
  application layer 152
  data link layer 152
  network layer 152
  physical layer 152
  presentation layer 152
  session Layer 152
  transport layer 152
  media layers 152
  OSI mnemonics used 152

P

penetration test
  common myths 78
  purpose 75
  VAPT 76
**Perimeter Intrusion Detection and
    Assessment System (PIDAS) 47**
perimeter security
  access control 47
  biometric devices 47
  Closed Circuit Television (CCTV) 47
  dogs 46
  fencing 47

R

Radio Frequency Interference(RFI) 50
reactive controls. *See* also corrective
    controls, administrative controls
red book 185
replay attacks 160
risk
    about 33, 35
    assets 34
    counter measures 36
    definitions 35
    impact 35
    risk assessment 36
    scenarios 36
    security violation 35
    threat 34
    threat agents 35
    vulnerability 35
risk, definitions
    risk acceptance 35
    risk analysis 35
    risk appetite 35
    risk assessment 35
    risk evaluation 35
    risk management 35
    risk treatment 35
risk assessment
    about 16, 37
    mitigation strategies 36
    qualitative risk assessment 37, 38
    quantitative risk assessment 37
    risk management 36
risk management
    purpose 15
roles, documented operating procedures
    operators 112
    security administrators 112
    security administrators, responsibilities 112
    system administrators 112
    system administrators, components 112
    system administrators, responsibilities 112
    users 113

S

Secret Key Cryptography. *See* SKC

Secure Hash Algorithm (SHA) 88
Secure Sockets Layer. *See* SSL, application
    layer protocols
security architecture and design
    knowledge requirements 175
    overview 183
    practice questions 181, 192
security awareness, requirements
    awareness needs, identifying 31
    awareness topics 31
    incident awareness, training 32
    ISO/IEC 27002 30
    measurement 33
    NIST publication 800-14 30
security awareness and training 29. *See*
    security awareness, requirements
security engineering practices,
    SSE-CMM 187
    PAO1 187
    PAO10 188
    PAO11 188
    PAO2 187
    PAO3 187
    PAO4 187
    PAO5 187
    PAO6 187
    PAO7 188
    PAO8 188
    PAO9 188
security management
    components 24
security management practices
    about 19
    authentication 21
    CIA Triad 20
    identification 21
    information security 19
    information security, assuring 21
security organizational process,
    SSE-CMM 188
    PA12 188
    PA13 188
    PA14 188
    PA15 188
    PA16 188
    PA17 189
    PA18 189

Thank you for buying
CISSP in 21 Days

About Packt Publishing

Packt, pronounced 'packed', published its first book *"Mastering phpMyAdmin for Effective MySQL Management"* in April 2004 and subsequently continued to specialize in publishing highly focused books on specific technologies and solutions.

Our books and publications share the experiences of your fellow IT professionals in adapting and customizing today's systems, applications, and frameworks. Our solution based books give you the knowledge and power to customize the software and technologies you're using to get the job done. Packt books are more specific and less general than the IT books you have seen in the past. Our unique business model allows us to bring you more focused information, giving you more of what you need to know, and less of what you don't.

Packt is a modern, yet unique publishing company, which focuses on producing quality, cutting-edge books for communities of developers, administrators, and newbies alike. For more information, please visit our website: www.packtpub.com.

Writing for Packt

We welcome all inquiries from people who are interested in authoring. Book proposals should be sent to author@packtpub.com. If your book idea is still at an early stage and you would like to discuss it first before writing a formal book proposal, contact us; one of our commissioning editors will get in touch with you.

We're not just looking for published authors; if you have strong technical skills but no writing experience, our experienced editors can help you develop a writing career, or simply get some additional reward for your expertise.

Zenoss Core Network and System Monitoring

ISBN: 978-1-847194-28-2   Paperback: 261 pages

A step-by-step guide to configuring, using, and adapting this free Open Source network monitoring system - with a Foreword by Mark R. Hinkle, VP of Community Zenoss Inc.

1. Discover, manage, and monitor IT resources

2. Build custom event processing and alerting rules

3. Configure Zenoss Core via an easy to use web interface

4. Drag and drop dashboard portlets with Google Maps integration

Configuring IPCop Firewalls

ISBN: 1-904811-36-1   Paperback: 154 pages

How to setup, configure and manage your Linux firewall, web proxy, DHCP, DNS, time server, and VPN with this powerful Open Source solution

1. Learn how to install, configure, and set up IPCop on your Linux servers

2. Use IPCop as a web proxy, DHCP, DNS, time server, and VPN

3. Advanced add-on management

Please check **www.PacktPub.com** for information on our titles

Designing and Implementing Linux Firewalls and QoS using netfilter, iproute2, NAT and l7-filter

ISBN: 1-904811-65-5   Paperback: 280 pages

Learn how to secure your system and implement QoS
using real-world scenarios for networks of all sizes

1. Implementing Packet filtering, NAT, bandwidth
   shaping, packet prioritization using netfilter/
   iptables, iproute2, Class Based Queuing (CBQ)
   and Hierarchical Token Bucket (HTB)

2. Designing and implementing 5 real-world
   firewalls and QoS scenarios ranging from small
   SOHO offices to a large scale ISP network that
   spans many cities

3. Building intelligent networks by marking,
   queuing, and prioritizing different types
   of traffic

OpenVPN

ISBN: 1-904811-85-X   Paperback: 258 pages

Learn how to build secure VPNs using this powerful
Open Source application

1. Learn how to install, configure, and create
   tunnels with OpenVPN on Linux, Windows,
   and MacOSX

2. Use OpenVPN with DHCP, routers, firewall,
   and HTTP proxy servers

3. Advanced management of security certificates

Please check **www.PacktPub.com** for information on our titles

Printed in the United Kingdom
by Lightning Source UK Ltd.
136249UK00001B/305/P